BASICS OF COMPUTERIZED ACCOUNTING

DR ANSHUMALI PANDEY

Made with ♥ on the Notion Press Platform
www.notionpress.com

Contents

Foreword

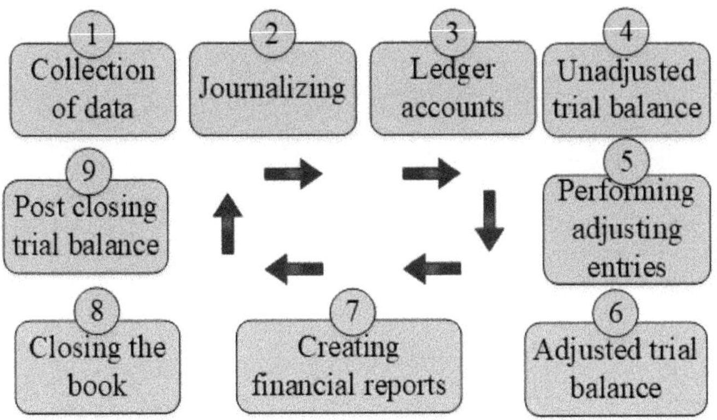

(Accounting Cycle)

Prologue

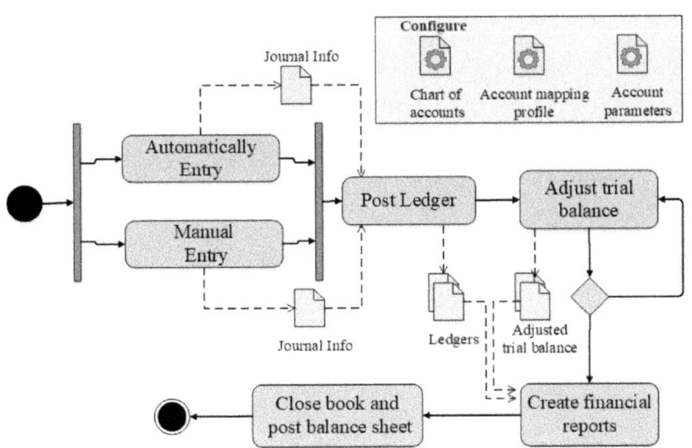

(Computerized Accounting)

CHAPTER ONE

Computerized Accounting - Introduction

Meaning of Computerized Accounting

A computerized accounting system saves a great deal of time and effort, considerably reduces (if not *eliminates*) mathematical errors, and allows for much more timely information than does a manual system. In a real-time environment, accounts are accessed and updated immediately to reflect activity, thus combining steps 2 and 3 as discussed in the preceding section. The need to test for equality of debits and credits through trial balances is usually not required in a computerized system accounting since most systems test for equality of debit and credit amounts as they are entered. If someone were to attempt to input data containing an inequality, the system would not accept the input. Since the computer is programmed to post amounts to the various accounts and calculate the new balances as new entries are made, the possibility of mathematical error is reduced.

Computers may also be programmed to record some adjustments automatically at the end of the period. Most software programs are also able to prepare the financial statement once it has been determined the account balances are correct. The closing process at the end of the period can also be done automatically by the computer.

Human judgment is still required to analyze the data for entry into the computer system correctly. Additionally, the accountant's knowledge and judgment are frequently required to determine the adjustments that are needed at the end of the reporting period. The mechanics of the system, however, can easily be handled by the computer.

Implementation of Accounting Cycle in Computerized Accounting

The primary objectives of the accounting function in an organization are to process financial information and to prepare financial statements at the end of the accounting period. Companies must systematically process financial information and must have staff who prepare financial statements on a monthly, quarterly, and/or annual basis. To meet these primary objectives, a series of steps is required. Collectively these steps are known as the *accounting cycle.* The steps, applicable to a manual accounting system, are described below. Later, there will be a brief discussion of a computerized processing system.

The Steps of the Cycle

1. ***Collect and analyze data from transactions and events:*** As transactions and events related to financial resources occur, they are analyzed with respect to their effect on

the financial position of the company. As an example, consider the sales for a day in a retail establishment that are collected on a cash register tape. These sales become inputs into the accounting system. Every organization establishes a chart of accounts that identifies the categories for recording transactions and events. The chart of accounts for the retail establishment mentioned earlier in this paragraph will include *Cash* and *Sales*.

2. ***Journalize transactions:*** After collecting and analyzing the information obtained in the first step, the information is entered in the *general journal*, which is called the *book of original entry*. Journalizing transactions may be done continually, but this step can de done in a batch at the end of the day if data from similar transactions are being sorted and collected, on a cash register tape, for example. At the end of the day, the sales of $4,000 for cash would be recorded in the general journal in this form:Cash 4000 Sales 4000
3. ***Post to general ledger:*** The general journal entries are posted to the, which is organized by *account*. All transactions for the same account are collected and summarized; for example, the account entitled "Sales" will accumulate the total value of the sales for the period. If posting were done daily, the "Sales" account in the would show the total sales for each day as well as the sales for the period to date. Posting to ledger accounts may be less frequent, perhaps at the end of each day, at the end of the week, or possibly even at the end of the month.
4. ***Prepare an unadjusted trial balance:*** At the end of the period, double-entry accounting requires that debits and credits recorded in the general ledger be equal. *Debit* and *credit* merely balances (e.g., assets and

expenses) and other accounts have credit balances (e.g., liabilities, owners' equity and revenues). As transactions are recorded in the general journal and subsequently posted to the ledger, all amounts recorded on the debit side of accounts (i.e., recorded on the left side) must equal all amounts recorded on the credit side of accounts (i.e., recorded on the right side). Preparing an tests the equality of debits and credits as recorded in the general ledger. If unequal amounts of debits and credits are found in this step, the reason for the is investigated and corrected before proceeding to the next step. Additionally, this trial balance provides the balances of all the accounts that may require adjustment in the next step.

1. ***Prepare adjustments:*** Period-end adjustments are required to bring accounts to their proper balances after considering transactions and/or events not yet recorded. Under accrual accounting, revenue is recorded when earned and expenses when incurred. Thus, an entry may be required at the end of the period to record revenue that has been earned but not yet recorded on the books. Similarly, an adjustment may be required to record an expense that may have been incurred but not yet recorded.
2. ***Prepare an adjusted trial balance:*** As with an unadjusted trial balance, this step tests the equality of debits and credits. However, assets, liabilities, owners' equity, revenues, and expenses will now reflect the adjustments that have been made in the previous step. If there should be amounts of debits and credits or if an account appears to be incorrect, or error is investigated and corrected.

3. ***Prepare financial statements:*** Financial statements are prepared using the corrected balances from the adjusted trial balance. These are one of the primary *outputs* of the financial accounting system.
4. ***Close the accounts:*** Revenues and expenses are accumulated and reported by period, either a monthly, quarterly, or yearly. To prevent their not being added to or comingled with revenues and expenses of another period, they need to be closed out—that is, given zero balances—at the end of each period. Their *net* balances, which represent the income or loss for the period, are transferred into owners' equity. Once revenue and expense accounts are closed, the only accounts that have balances are the asset, liability, and owners' equity accounts. Their balances are carried forward to the next period.
5. ***Prepare a post-closing trial balance:*** The purpose of this final step is two-fold: to determine that all revenue and expense accounts have been closed properly and to test the equality of debit and credit balances of all the balance sheet accounts, that is, assets, liabilities and owners' equity.

Old methods and machines used in accounting

The most common method of keeping the financial records of a company was manually. A bookkeeper kept the journals, the accounts receivable, the accounts payable and the ledgers in his best possible penmanship. In later years, an accounting machine, which was capable of performing normal bookkeeping functions, such as tabulating in vertical columns, performing arithmetic functions, and typing horizontal rows was used. The billing machine, which was designed to typewrite names, addresses, and descriptions, to multiply and extend, to compute discounts, and to add net total, posting the requisite data to the proper accounts, and so to prepare a customer's bill automatically once the operator has entered the necessary information, was used. Early accounting machines were marvels of mechanical complexity, often combining a typewriter and various kinds of calculator elements. The refinements in speed and capacity made possible by advances in electronics and operating complexity of these machines. Many of the newer "generations" of accounting machines are operated by a computer to which they are permanently connected.

Basics of computerized accounting

Because of the minute by minute change in finances, accurate record keeping is critical. Computerizing a business's general ledger, payroll, and other accounting tasks increases office efficiency. With a computer, you can request and receive an in house balance sheet, an income statement, or other accounting reports at a moment's notice. While keeping your checkbook on a computer may not be practical, computers are great for handling complex home financial records. You can get statements on net worth and year's tax deductible expenses within minutes.

A. Spreadsheets

Electronic spreadsheets allow you to do anything that you would normally do with a calculator, pencil and columnar scratch pad. Spreadsheets were primarily designed for managers who in the process of planning must do "what if" calculations. Due to their flexibility, electronic spreadsheets have found their way into small businesses and, to a lesser extent to homes. A typical integrated double entry accounting system will contain some or all of the following components: accounts receivable, accounts payable, general ledger, inventory, order entry, payroll, time, and billing.

It takes its name from the accountant's spreadsheet—a sheet of paper with rules for rows and columns—on which such work was usually done. Spreadsheet programs are much faster, more accurate, and easier to use than traditional accounting techniques. The programs are widely used on personal computers for keeping sales, expense and inventory records, and for budgeting and forecasting future sales and expenses. As a result of these and many other applications, computer spreadsheets have become the most important of all software tools for modern businesses.

Early programs such as VisiCalc provided 254 rows and 63 columns for entering data and formulas for calculations. Some modern programs for computers with large memories provide thousands of rows and hundreds of columns. VisiCalc was introduced by Robert Frankston, a young computer programmer, and Dan Bricklin, a Harvard

Business School student who was looking for a way to use the power of a computer to simplify complex time-consuming financial analyses. VisiCalc proved so useful in such applications that it provided an entry for personal computers into the business world. In 1980, the Sorcim Corporation introduced SuperCalc, a similar spreadsheet program for personal computers using the CPM operating system.

A new generation of computer software for business began with integrated spreadsheet programs, which can be used to prepare spreadsheets, create graphs, and manage data. In such programs, for example, it is easy to display spreadsheet data in the form of a graph or to transfer data from a data base to a spreadsheet. One of the first such programs was Lotus 1-2-3, an immediate success following its introduction in 1983.

In the third generation of integrated business software, spreadsheet, graphics, and data management capabilities were supplemented by word processing and communications capabilities. With such comprehensive programs, it became possible to create multiple windows on the computer display. Each window could contain a different application—a graph in one, a spreadsheet in another, and word processing in a third. The window capabilities of integrated programs such as Symphony and Framework make it easy, for example, to transfer a spreadsheet or a data-base report to word processing for styling and formatting before printing.

B. **General Ledger**

General Ledger is a labor saving device for the preparation of financial statements and for establishing multiple income and cost entries.

C. **Accounts Receivable**

Accounts receivable, when computerized, can get your bills out the same day you've performed a service. An accounts receivable module prepares invoices and customer accounts, adds credit charges where appropriate, handles incoming payments, flags your attention to customers that are delinquent, and produces dunning notices. It allows you to have daily cash control. You get out the bills on time, yet you avoid errors such as billing a customer twice for the same item. The further advantage is that debits and credits are posted automatically to the general ledger, order entry, and in some instances inventory, once they are entered in accounts receivable.

D. **Accounts Payable**

Accounts payable, when computerized, will provide for purchase order control, invoice processing, payment selection and handling, check writing and control, cash-requirements, forecasting, and Form 1099 preparation. It will also double-check the accuracy of the vendor's invoice, and some software systems will cross-check it against the purchase order and the inventory module.

E. **Inventory Control**

Inventory Control module has multiple functions, including tracking inventory for both costing and tax purposes, controlling purchasing (and the overall level of expenditure) and minimizing the investment in inventory (and subsequent loss of cash flow). The payroll module prepares and prints payroll checks, including all itemized deductions. It is integrated with the general ledger so you automatically set aside the correct amount for FICA and withholding.

F. Point of Sale

Point of sale module captures all sales information at (or in place of) the cash register, including salesperson, date, customer, credit information, items, and quantity sold. It can produce sales slips or sales invoices, plus it reports on items, customer, and salesperson activity.

G. Purchasing and Receiving

Purchasing and receiving module can represent an invaluable addition. It can generate purchase orders and track their fulfillment. You can find out which vendors are delivering on time and saving you the expense of having to follow up on partial and incomplete orders.

H. Time and Billing Module

Time and billing module reduces manual and clerical work, simplifies the billing process, prompts you and your partners to bill on time, reduces unbilled work-in progress, minimizes unreported time, reduces unbilled time, measures and analyzes nonchargeable time and provides criteria to analyze staff performance. Because a computerized accounting system is basically a computerized data management system, the disposition of labor is almost the same. One staff member must serve as a data-base manager and be in charge of setting up the chart of accounts, establishing the interrelationships among the files and establishing and maintaining an audit trail.

CHAPTER TWO

Computerized Processing Systems

Computerized Processing Systems:

Accounting software: You probably noticed that much of the material in this chapter involves rather mundane processing. Once the initial journal entry is prepared, the data are merely being manipulated to produce the ledger, trial balance, and financial statements. No wonder, then, that some of the first business applications that were computerized many years ago related to transaction processing. In short, the only "analytics" relate to the initial transaction recordation. All of the subsequent steps are merely mechanical, and are aptly suited to computerization.

How much does it cost: Many companies produce accounting software. These packages range from the simple to the complex. Some basic products for a small business may be purchased for under $100. In large organizations, millions may be spent hiring consultants to install large enterprise-wide packages. Recently, some software companies have even offered accounting systems maintained on their own network, with the customers utilizing the internet to enter data and produce their reports.

What do they look like: As you might expect, the look, feel, and function of software-based packages varies significantly. Each company's product must be studied to understand its unique attributes. But, in general, accounting software packages:

1. Attempt to simplify and automate data entry (e.g., a point-of-sale terminal may actually become a data entry device so that sales are automatically "booked" into the accounting system as they occur).
2. Frequently divide the accounting process into modules related to functional areas such as sales/collection, purchasing/payment, and others.
3. Attempt to be "user-friendly" by providing data entry blanks that are easily understood in relation to the underlying transactions.
4. Attempt to minimize key-stokes by using "pick lists," automatic call-up functions, and auto-complete type technology.
5. Are built on data-base logic, allowing transaction data to be sorted and processed based on any query structure (e.g., produce an income statement for July, provide a listing of sales to Customer Smith, etc.)
6. Provide up-to-date data that may be accessed by key business decision makers.
7. Are capable of producing numerous specialized reports in addition to the key financial statements.

Advantages of using the computer in accounting

The most important advantage of using the computer is the speed with which we can get Accounting done. In addition, we find that it is very easy to do accounting functions. Posting to the ledger, a tedious task of double entry, when done directly from the general ledger module, can be largely automated when done through special purpose modules like accounts payable or accounts receivable. With an accounts receivable module, you just need to enter the actual cash totals of items purchased and the software distributes these amounts to the general ledger so they become credits to corresponding revenue accounts. At the same time, an offsetting entry is made automatically to the accounts receivable account.

With a computer, one can receive a balance sheet, income statement or other accounting reports at a moment's notice. We also find that some day to day data entry can be turned over to relatively unskilled workers.

Disadvantages of using the computer in accounting

When you use a computer, it is possible that data can be lost because of hardware or software damage. Since the computer has no judgement of its own, it does not pick up on errors as a human being does. There can be loss of data due to accidents like fire etc.. There can be loss of data or change of data due to fraud or embezzlement. There can be loss or unavailability of data due to loss of staff. Inaccurate data may be due to clerical error or mistakes in programming. Total security is economically unachievable and some failures must be expected. The right level of expenditure on security measures will minimize the sum of the cost of the measures and the expected loss. There will always be some risks that are best shared through insurance, rather than prevented or avoided.

Much computer-related crime is opportunist: people who were not seeking any advantage had temptation thrust under their noses. Copies of computer printouts get mis-directed, or thrown in a waste paper basket in a public place. Magnetic tapes from bankrupt companies have been sold with data still on them. Often a programming error reveals a system flaw: someone who by chance reads a magnetic tape file that he should have been writing discovers interesting data on it.

Sabotage, vandalism, malicious damage, and arson tend to be even more destructive than the Acts of God they emulate. Political and industrial action, riots and civil commotions, may not be aimed specifically at the computer but they can be very effective in preventing its operation.

Fraud and embezzlement are usually achieved on a computer system by altering data or programs. There are numerous techniques, varying from additions and deletions to input data, through changing the standing information files, modifying the behavior of programs, to duplicating or suppressing output. Although most frauds that have been reported had gone on for some time, it could be that 'one shot' frauds have been more frequent but more often escape detection.

Eavesdropping and stealing information by tapping telecommunications lines requires the sort of technical skill which is very widely available (to the surprise of those without technical education). It is possible to emulate a legitimate user of a system, or discover his password through trickery or as the result of carelessness, and thus have access to the information he would have, such access can be very important for setting up more profitable operations, such as taking money out of little used bank accounts, or concealing changes made in files. There are other ways of trespassing, without using wire tapping. For example, the magnetically encoded cards often used as keys to systems can be copies and altered, giving the villain access to credit, cash or other valuable assets.

Wherever a computer is used to handle an organization's accounts, it can be used as a means of attacking the funds it controls. In most computerized bookkeeping systems, it is the computer which effectively causes credit transfer; so by establishing false accounts, or diverting some of the contents of the real ones, credit can reach a false beneficiary. The system can also be used to conceal a change in the cost, or the illegitimate acquisition or the destruction of tangible goods and services.

CHAPTER THREE

Concept of Accounting Groups

What is Group?

The conceptual underpinning for answering this question is an important issue in understanding the principles of a group. Basically there are some basic concepts for accounting groups which are described below :

1. ***The Parent Company Concept***: It emphasizes legal control and assumes that it is for the equity investors of the parent company that the Group accounts are prepared and to whom a true and fair view must be disclosed. This concept makes no attempt to disclose a true an fair view to any minority shareholders in the subsidiary companies or to other interested parties. It assumes that a group consists of a parent company which dominates a number of dependent or subsidiary companies by the exercise of the voting power vested in the ordinary shareholders. In other words, dominance

or control, is established by the existence of the power to exercise control, rather than actual exercise of control. This legal form is given precedence over the commercial substance.

2. ***The Entity Concept :*** The entity concept emphaises de facto control and is based on the economic unit. It is founded on the principle that Group comprises a number of entities drawn together usually by unified management or the actual exercise of control into an economic unit. It gives equal importance to all shareholders, whether majority or minority. This way of looking the group is probably more appropriate for such users as employees and managers. This concept can also cover the case of unified management where there are directors in common to a nmber of companies who act in the interest of other companies of which they are directors.

Methods of accounting for a "group" have evolved and include the following:

- Cost method
- Equity method
- Acquisition method
- Proportional accounting
- Aggregate accounting
- Merger accounting

Accounting groups may comprise accounting, management accounting, financial reporting, auditing and taxation.

Management accounting group cluster around five themes:

- Management by accounting
- Performance management
- Costing systems
- Financial modeling
- Accounting profession and accounting education.

Financial reporting group has a strong public policy dimension, focusing on auditing and the regulation of corporate reporting and taxation, from contemporary, historical and international perspectives. It includes:

- Audit sampling
- The conceptual framework of financial reporting
- The history of accounting from feudalism to financial reporting in 19th-century Britain
- The identification and measurement of marketing assets
- Short-termism
- Creative accounting and financial services markets
- Comparative international accounting.

CHAPTER FOUR

Accounting Packages

There are various kinds of accounting packages available in the market. These softwares are designed and developed as per the requirement of the business / corporate. Few of these softwares cater to particular industry and few of these softwares are generic like Tally etc. Depending on the size of the business and nature of the business these accounting packages can have several types of classification. Let's study these classifications in detail:

Custom Tailored vs. Standardized packages:

Many of the small business require basic level of accounting which involves ledger, profit and loss account, cash book, vouchers etc. This type of need is catered by the generic software which is called as *Standardized packages.* These packages are easy to use and can be easily implemented for SMEs as they share common set of functionalities of accounting. Packages like Tally are an excellent example of Standardized packages. But for big companies or business that have specific requirement of accounting deals require an accounting package that could cater their specific needs. So to cater that group software companies develop customized accounting packages or tailor their existing accounting package (ERP module) as per business requirement. Custom / Tailored packages are more flexible than standardized packages. Usually custom / tailored package cost more than standardized packages

Single vs. Multiple user:

For the companies which are small in operations and require only basis level of accounting, usually desktop based application based software serve their purpose which have single user. Single user accounting packages have only basic set of functionalities of accounts and less scalable. Packages like busy are single user based accounting package. Big companies which operate at multi locations require accounting package which could be installed at multiple locations and could be operated by multiple users at the same and all the accounting data could be stored in one location. These multi user packages are web based application and always require internet connectivity. These are highly scalable and require huge infrastructure

Overview of Standard Accounting Packages : GNUCash – AN *OPEN SOURCE ACCOUNTING SOFTWARE*

GnuCash is personal and small-business financial-accounting software, freely licensed under the http://www.gnu.org GPL and available for GNU/Linux, BSD, Solaris, Mac OS X and Microsoft Windows.

Designed to be easy to use, yet powerful and flexible, GnuCash allows you to track bank accounts, stocks, income and expenses. As quick and intuitive to use as a checkbook register, it is based on professional accounting principles to ensure balanced books and accurate reports.

Feature Highlights

- Double-Entry Accounting
- Stock/Bond/Mutual Fund Accounts
- Small-Business Accounting
- Customers, Vendors, Jobs, Invoices, A/P, A/R
- QIF/OFX/HBCI Import, Transaction Matching
- Reports, Graphs
- Scheduled Transactions
- Financial Calculations

Features:

Checkbook-Style Register

The checkbook-style register provides a custom, convenient and familiar interface to entering financial transactions. The register supports common checking and credit-card transactions, as well as income, stock and currency transactions

Double Entry

Every transaction must debit one account and credit others by an equal amount. This ensures that the "books balance": that the difference between income and outflow exactly equals the sum of all assets and equity.

Reports, Graphs

GnuCash has an integrated reporting and graphing module, and comes complete with a full suite of standard and customizeable reports, such as Balance Sheet, Profit & Loss, Portfolio Valuation, and many others.

Income/Expense Account Types

Income/Expense Account Types (Categories) allow you to categorize your cash flow. When used properly with the double-entry feature and equity accounts, these enable you to generate reports, such as Profit & Loss, that plain-vanilla systems cannot handle.

Multiple Currencies

Different accounts can be denominated in different currencies. Currency movements between accounts are fully balanced when double-entry is enabled.

Stock/Mutual Fund Portfolios

Track stocks individually (one per account) or in portfolio of accounts (a group of accounts that can be displayed together).

Small Business Accounting Features

Simplify managing a small business with Customer and Vendor tracking, Invoicing and Bill Payment, and Tax and Billing Terms.

QIF Import

Intuit® Quicken® QIF files can be imported, and are automatically merged to eliminate duplicate transactions.

OFX Import

GnuCash is the first free software application to support the Open Financial Exchange protocol that many banks and financial services are starting to use.

HBCI Support

GnuCash is the first free software application to support the German Home Banking Computer Information protocol, allowing German users to perform statement download and initiate bank transfers and direct debits.

Improved Import Transaction Matching

The development of OFX and HBCI support has also resulted in an improved transaction matching system that more accurately recognizes duplicate transactions during file import.

Statement Reconciliation

A reconcile window with running reconciled and cleared balances makes balancing against bank statements easy.

General Ledger

Multiple accounts can be displayed in one register window at the same time. This can ease the trouble of tracking down typing/entry errors. It also provides a convenient way of viewing a portfolio of many stocks, by showing all transactions in that portfolio.

Online Stock & Mutual Fund Quotes

Get Stock & Mutual Fund quotes from various web sites, update portfolio automatically. Additional pricing sources are added regularly.

Check Printing

Checks may be printed in standard formats on common check stocks. A customization GUI allows custom check layouts to be developed.

Scheduled Transactions

You can now create recurring transactions, including automatic reminders when a transaction is due, the ability to postpone a scheduled transaction without canceling it, and the ability to specify only a limited number of transactions.

Mortgage & Loan Repayment Druid

A guided dialogue for setting up loan payments as scheduled transactions.

New User Manual and Help

A new help subsystem that focuses on how to do tasks is now available, in addition to a Tutorial and Concepts guide that gives the user background information on accounting principles and how they are reflected in GnuCash.

Localization:

Handles internationalized dates and currencies. The Gnucash menus and popups have been translated to 21 languages, including Chinese, Danish, French, German,

Hungarian, Italian, Japanese, Norwegian, Polish, Portuguese, Russian, Spanish, Swedish, Turkish, Ukrainian, and British English. Documentation is available in English, French, Portuguese and Spanish.

CHAPTER FIVE

Hierarchy of Accounts

> "*Whatever your actual percentages, it's helpful to divide your accounts into three categories. In the hierarchy of accounts, perhaps 10 percent of the companies would be considered* ***strategic accounts****. The next tier consists of your normal* ***customer / Normal accounts*** *might account for 30 percent of your total customer base, and the remaining 60 percent would consist of your* ***prospects i.e. Prospect account***"

Lorose

Generating Account Hierarchies

Data aggregation is available via the Roll-up views provided the administrator defines one or more hierarchies. In accounting softwares, the application administrator typically defines a "default" hierarchy by associating accounts with one another using the parent field on a company form, or the subaccount view for child accounts. Administrators can define account hierarchies display aggregated data—the activities, opportunities, contacts, and coverage teams—across account organizational structures. For example, the top node of the hierarchy contains activities for the organization, the subsidiaries below the organization, the departments at the subsidiaries, and contacts working at any level of the tree. As the end users move up and down the tree, they see more or less data rolled up to the selected level.

In most of the accounting softwares like Sibel tools, Application administrator can define two types of hierarchies for data aggregation—a default hierarchy for all end users and specific hierarchies that are used only by certain end users.

Default Account Hierarchies

The application administrator sets up a default account hierarchy once, during the initial application setup. The default hierarchy is available to all end users who are not tied to a specific hierarchy and who have been granted view access to the accounts represented in the hierarchy. It is the administrator's responsibility to give end user access to Account views. For more information, see Applications Administration Guide.

When new accounts are added, they are automatically added to the default hierarchy tree and the contacts, coverage teams, activities, and opportunities that are associated with the accounts are automatically displayed in the rollup views.

In the preconfigured application, using the Generate Hierarchy button adds only parent account and child accounts to the hierarchy. Any account that does not have a child or parent is not displayed in the rollup views. In *Siebel Tools*, you can change the *DynHierarchy Load All Accounts* user property to alter this behavior.

The *DynHierarchy Load All Accounts* user property on the Dynamic Hierarchy Direct Relationship business component can be set to N or Y. When it is set to N, only parent and children appear in the generated hierarchy. When DynHierarchy Load All Accounts user property is set to Y, all accounts are added to the account hierarchy. For information on setting user properties, see Siebel Tools Reference.

To generate a default account hierarchy

1. In the application-level menu, choose View>Site Map>Application Administration> Account Hierarchies.
2. In the Account Hierarchies list, click Generate Hierarchy.

The parent-child account relationships that have been defined in your application are registered for participation in the roll-up views. This process may take some time, depending on the quantity of account records that are in your existing environment.

When the account hierarchy has been generated, a new record appears in the Account Hierarchies list. The Hierarchy Name field of the record contains the user Id of the administrator who generated the account hierarchy and the time it was generated. If it is the only account hierarchy record, the Default field is automatically checked. The accounts that have been added for participation in the roll-up views appear in the Account Relationships list.

NOTE: If no accounts are visible in the Account Relationships list, click the query button, step off the query, and click Go to refresh the view.

1. Optional. Rename the account hierarchy and, if necessary, check the Default field.

NOTE: If end users are using the application when you generate the account hierarchy, they must log off and log on again to see the default account hierarchy in the rollup views.

Dynamic Account Hierarchies

In some cases, users work with particular accounts or subaccounts of a large corporation, but not with others. In these instances, some end users do not need to or should not see aggregated data across the entire corporation. An administrator can define a custom hierarchical structure across which data can be aggregated. This defined structure, called a dynamic hierarchy, can be as simple or complex as needed and offers users the ability to aggregate data across the accounts they are interested in seeing.

To create a dynamic account hierarchy of selected accounts

1. In the application-level menu, choose View > Site Map > Application Administration > Account Hierarchies.
2. Create a new account hierarchy record.
3. Click the add button in the Account Relationships list, select accounts in the Add Account dialog box, and click OK.All the accounts in the Account Relationship list belong to the new account hierarchy.
4. To define parent and child relationships, select an account in the Account Relationship list that has no parent account, click the select button in the Parent Account field, and select a parent account in the Pick Parent Account dialog box.
5. Repeat Step 4 for all accounts that have no parents.
6. Associate the dynamic hierarchy with an organization.

End users can only see the account hierarchy with which their current position's primary organization is tied. It is the administrator's responsibility to associate end users with positions, positions with organizations, and organizations with hierarchies.

New Account Hierarchy Setup in GNU cash:

This druid helps you to create a set of GnuCash accounts. It will appear if you choose Create a new set of accounts in the Welcome to GnuCash! menu.

To start this druid manually go to File -> New File. This will create a new blank GnuCash file and then automatically start the New Account Hierarchy Setup druid.

The New Account Hierarchy Setup druid opens with a screen that briefly describes what this druid does. The three buttons at the very bottom of the screen will not change while using the druid.

- The Cancel button is used to exit the druid and cancel creating a new set of accounts. Any selections you have made in this druid up to this point will be lost.
- The Back button will bring up the previous screen so you can change a selection made on that screen.

    - The Forward button will bring up the next screen so you can continue though the druid.

The next screen allows you to select the default currency to use for your accounts. The Select... button on this screen is used to access the list of currencies. The Select... button brings up the Select currency/security dialog.

- The Type: drop down list defaults to CURRENCY. Other types are used for setting up commodities for stock related accounts.
- The Currency/security: drop down list defaults to USD (US Dollar). If you wish your accounts to use a different default currency select one from the list.
- The OK button is used to confirm your selection.
- The New... button brings up the New Currency/ Security dialog. This is used for setting up commodities for stock related accounts.
- The Cancel button is used to exit the dialog without using any changes you have made.

The next screen is used to choose a *hierarchy of accounts* to create. You will see a screen divided into three parts.

- The top part has a list of Account Types and Descriptions for commonly used hierarchies of accounts. Select from this list the types of accounts you wish to use. You can select as many types of accounts as you wish.
- The left bottom part has a Detailed Description of the account type you selected.
- The right bottom part has a list of the Accounts that will be created from the selected account type.
- The Select All button allows you to include all of the account types from the top part.
- The Clear All button allows you to deselect all of the account types from the top part.

The next screen allows you to enter opening balances for your accounts and also select if the account is a placeholder account. Placeholder accounts are used to create a hierarchy of accounts and normally do not have transactions or opening balances. Equity accounts also do not have opening balances.

- The left side of the screen has a list of Account Names. Select each account to enter a opening balance or to make it a placeholder account.

- The right side of the screen has a checkbox to make an account a Placeholder and a box to add the Opening Balance for the selected account.

The last screen gives you a list of three choices to finish the druid.

- The Cancel button is used to exit the druid and cancel creating a new set of accounts. Any selections you have made in this druid up to this point will be lost.
- The Back button will bring up the previous screen so you can change a selection made on that screen.
- The Finish button creates the accounts you have selected.

You should now have a hierarchy of accounts in your main GnuCash account window.

CHAPTER SIX

Codification in Accounting

In January 15, 2008, The Financial Accounting Standards Board (FASB) officially launched the one-year verification phase of the FASB Accounting Standards Codification (Codification). During the verification period, constituents are encouraged to use the online Codification Research System free of charge to research accounting issues and provide feedback on whether the Codification content accurately reflects existing U.S. generally accepted accounting principles (GAAP) for nongovernmental entities. Users are advised that the Codification content is not yet approved as authoritative and, therefore, they must verify research results using their existing resources for the currently effective literature.

After addressing the issues raised during the constituent feedback process, the FASB is expected to formally approve the Codification as the single source of authoritative U.S. GAAP, other than guidance issued by the Securities and Exchange Commission (SEC). To improve usability, the Codification will include authoritative content issued by the SEC, as well as selected SEC staff interpretations. Upon approval by the FASB, all accounting standards (other than the SEC guidance) used to populate the Codification will be superseded. At that time, with the exception of any SEC or grandfathered guidance, all other accounting literature not included in the Codification will become non-authoritative.

Users who register at http://asc.fasb.org are able to review the Codification free of charge and provide specific content-related feedback at the individual paragraph level as well as general system-related feedback. During the verification period, Codification content will be updated for changes resulting from constituent feedback and new standards.

The Codification includes all accounting standards issued by a standard-setter within levels A through D of the current U.S. GAAP hierarchy, including FASB, American Institute of Certified Public Accountants (AICPA), Emerging Issues Task Force (EITF), and related literature.

The Codification does not change GAAP; instead it reorganizes the thousands of U.S. GAAP pronouncements into roughly 90 accounting topics, and displays all topics using a consistent structure. The SEC guidance will follow a similar topical structure in separate SEC sections.

The FASB expects that the new structure and new system will:

- Reduce the amount of time and effort required to solve an accounting research issue.
- Improve usability of the literature thereby mitigating the risk of noncompliance with standards.
- Provide real-time updates as new standards are released.

- Assist the FASB with the research and convergence efforts required during the standard- setting process.
- Become the authoritative source of literature for the completed XBRL taxonomy.

The home page of the Codification Research System includes various items that users should be aware of, including:

- A suggested approach for verifying the Codification content.
- A Notice to Constituents that describes Codification-related matters, including content matters for constituent feedback. For example, the Notice addresses the standards and elevated guidance used to populate the Codification, the use of December 31, 2008, as the authoring effective date, and conflicts resolved by Board decision for which the Board is requesting feedback.
- Content excluded from the Codification Research System on the verification launch date. The FASB expects to release such content shortly after the initial launch.

The Codification Research System also includes general information about how to use the online research system and special features such as Cross Reference Reports (to locate where standards reside), Join Sections (to join similar Sections from multiple Topics and Subtopics into a single document), and Go To (to jump directly to a specific Topic, Subtopic, Section, or paragraph).

The Accounting Standards Codification excludes governmental accounting standards.

CHAPTER SEVEN

Selection of a good Accounting package

There are many different types of accounting software packages and applications currently available today. To select the best accounting product you will first need to decide your individual and corporate needs. Small business accounting software functions much differently in many respects that accounting software manufactured as an enterprise resources planning solution for example.

If you are a large enterprise or firm you will want to investigate a comprehensive enterprise solution that offers multi-user capability. Some examples of popular software programs in this field include Oracle People Soft Enterprise One and mySAP All-in-One. If you are looking for a basic accounting software package you may opt for SAP Business One or Microsoft Great Plains software.

Small Business Software and Personal Accounting Software

Small businesses can usually get away with a more basic program like QuickBooks Enterprise or Professional or MS Small Business Financials. If you are looking for an accounting software application for personal use, a basic accounting software program like quicken or QuickBooks or even Peachtree should easily accommodate your every need. Most of these software programs come equipped with accounts payables, account receivables, payroll and general ledger features. Most will also generate basic reports, invoices and keep track of other expenses, assets and small financial items you may want to keep track of from day to day.

The primary difference between these smaller software applications and larger enterprise solutions is the smaller applications won't necessarily integrate to serve multiple operations like manufacturing, marketing and engineering. Most ordinary people or small businesses however will not need this capability in a software accounting package.

Best Small Business Accounting Software

Many small business owners feel that they don't require software for their organization as the quantum of work is small. When the time comes for paying the tax they invariably find themselves in trouble.

Small businesses run on limited resources financial as well as man-power. The software in such organizations should be chosen with care. Decision for the best small business accounting software should rest on features like smooth functioning, scalability and learning curve. However, all the software utility will not be availed successfully by a novice unless certain amount of self effort or training is put in by them.

Survey the market for the full spectrum of small business accounting software. Narrow down the range by selecting the possible small business accounting software. Call over the consultant of the software company to evaluate and understand what and how of the software.

At the back of your mind, just remember how the software will simplify your operations. Express your view clearly on what is being generated and how you want it. The generation and use of reports and tools should be user friendly. Assess it from the point of view of business strategy and internal organization.

Find out the software's connectivity with other office gadgets like printer, E-Commerce features and internet. System integration should be compatible with new applications.

Some software requires activation. Learn to unlock it with proper technique otherwise you will find yourself locked out.

Best small business accounting software should not be confused with personal accounting. Data entry screen is carbon copy of paper sheet and screen tips and drags and drop functionality makes it absolutely a child's play.

Make sure, you get an efficient time after sale service from the company in times of break-down. The technical tips to be made available as and when they occur.

Microsoft Dynamics GP

One of the medium levels accounting software that has come up from the Microsoft stable is the Microsoft Dynamics GP. In fact, it is an integrated, world-class financial and business management solution. It easily connects people and processes from all areas of the business. It is designed to easily integrate with the look and feel of the Microsoft Office programs. If you are looking to upgrade from basic accounting software, this is the product for you.

Microsoft Dynamics GP is composed of features and functionality that allow you to better manage finances, sales, purchasing, inventory, CRM, payroll, reporting and more. You can easily streamline your business processes, improve business insight, and accelerate the productivity and more.

If you want a financial management system that integrates with your existing Microsoft Dynamics CRM, Microsoft Dynamics GP is the answer. Combination the above two, you can provide yourself with tools that are needed for a richer and more supported experience.

The main benefits of the Microsoft Dynamics GP are discussed below;

1. Microsoft Dynamics GP provides functionality for finances, analytics and reporting, project management, inventory and order processing, e-commerce and more.
2. Microsoft Dynamics GP enhances reporting capabilities. Enhanced reporting capabilities let your clients view data and publish reports on a recurring basis.
3. Effective inventory and distribution management from Microsoft Dynamics GP will help you in delivering

superior customer service with powerful inventory, distribution and order management capabilities.

4. You can easily streamline your business operations and will enable in collaboration among employees to save time and resources.
5. Microsoft Dynamics GP is at once cost-effective and reliable and it is delivered by a vast network of trusted service providers and backed by extensive service and support.

All these benefits have made it clear to you about the usefulness of using the Microsoft Dynamics GP in your business. Another important use of Microsoft Dynamics GP is with the Microsoft Retail Management System. It connects data from the point-of-sale to the back office and through the supply chain. This means retailers can have improved visibility in sales transactions. The program also offers increased general-ledger visibility, which helps eliminate double entry, such as payouts, surcharges and manual inventory adjustments.

Small Business Accounting Software: A Way To Expand

Starting a business is not a cakewalk. Apart from developing and selling products and services, managing finances is essential for the smooth running of a business unit. That is why accounting is called the language of business.

The present day work pressures ask for unerring handling of finances and accounts. In case of small business houses, it is really important to be organized which is possibly only by adopting a good accounting software. Long-term financial goals of a business unit, requires effective management of accounting. All in all I would say your small business accounting software just lets you be the boss of your business. For, it is just not possible to have an error free accounting manually.

In business, it is important to know from where the funds will come and go. Doing this accounting work manually is certainly going to be cumbersome and will take a hell lot of time.

Broadly speaking the benefits of accounting software can be outlined as:

1. It helps you do your accounting tasks quickly. It assists you to run your business without any hiccups.
2. It provides you with 100 % correct reports and tools that makes your business accounting simple and help you manage financial data effectively.
3. You are able to manage the flow of cash in little time.
4. It is also possible for you to predict future bills, revenues and reports generating.

But before buying accounting software for your business, certain things like what are the functionalities you want in your software must be considered for sure.

You should look for user-friendly software. Your accounting software should resemble its traditional paper counterparts as it will help to run your software smoothly. You can explore the functionalities of the software if you are familiar with the layout.

E-commerce and Internet are also important for your small business. Look for software which combines all these features.

There are many benefits of accounting software and there are many accounting software in the market as well. And choosing the best software and learning about its benefits is tantamount to learning the benefits of a small business accounting software.

Consider Microsoft Office Small Business Accounting 2006, for instance. It is a brand in itself in the field of small business accounting software. It is a full-featured financial management program designed for companies with 25 or fewer employees.

Small business software analyzes financial data with customizable reports including Profit and Loss, Customer Transaction History, Reconciliation Detail, Check Detail, and more. You can easily judge the financial status of your business with it.

Built-in features of a small business software such as cash flow forecasting tools, payroll services help to control costs and manage risks. Most of the small businesses accounting software are exceptionally good. It is very hard to choose one or to choose the best. Microsoft Office Small Business Accounting 2006 and QuickBooks Accounting software are two really good software. For, they can easily synchronize with MAC OS without any difficulty.

Top Accounting Softwares in the market

Simply put, accounting is the lifeline of a business. Accounting deals with summarizing, analyzing and reporting the financial data and information about a business. An accounting software records and processes the accounting transactions of a business within its functional modules. Financial statements consisting of the balance sheet, profit and loss account, and statement of changes in financial position can be easily prepared with accounting software.

Accounting software is all about the various functional modules that it has. Some of them are- General ledger which takes care of the company's financial dealings; Accounts Payable where the company enters its bills and pays the money it owes; Accounts Receivable where money received is entered.

The different categories or types of accounting software are as follows:

a. Small business/personal accounting software which are mainly meant for home users. They are simple and inexpensive with simple functioning such as management of budgets.
b. Low end accounting software are for small business markets that are capable of serving a single national market. Such software are characterized by 'single entry' products.
c. Mid market accounting software are for companies with large businesses. These software are capable of serving the needs of multiple national accountancy standards and facilitate accounting in multiple currencies.
d. High end accounting software are complex and expensive business accounting software that are also known as Enterprise Resource Planning or ERP software.

However, you have to keep certain things in mind before buying an accounting software, like the prices of the software, its different features, its after-sales support and alike. Most of the accounting software include all the important accounting modules. The more specialized features a software has, the more expensive it becomes. Your software features must be compatible with your business. Also, the after-sales support is important like FAQ package, local service center and others.

There are a lot of top accounting software available in every category. So, it is not easy to select the best ones. Below are top five accounting software in every category.

A. Small business/personal accounting software:

1. ePeachtree (Best Software)
2. MYOB Plus for Windows (MYOB Software) 3.Peachtree Complete Accounting (Best Software) 4.QuickBooks Online (Intuit)

5.Small Business Manager (Microsoft)

A. Low-End Accounting Software:

1.BusinessVision 32 (Best Software) 2.MAS 90 & MAS 200 (Best Software) 3.QuickBooks Pro 2003 (Intuit)

4.ACCPAC Pro Series (ACCPAC International) 5.Vision Point 2000 (Best Software)

A. Middle-Market Accounting Software:

1.ACCPAC Advantage Series Corporate Edition (Best Software) 2.Great Plains (Microsoft) MAS 90 & MAS 200

(Best Software) 3.Navision (Microsoft)

4.SouthWare Excellence Series (SouthWare) 5.SYSPRO (SysproUSA)

A. High-end accounting ERP Market:

1.Axapta (Microsoft Software) 2.e-Business Suite (Oracle) 3.MAS 500 (Best Software).

1. Solomon (Microsoft)
2. ACCPAC Advantage Series Enterprise Edition (Best Software)

In compiling the above list, a variety of factors such as feedbacks from customers, scalability of the software, and after-sales support are used. Also, the different attributes for different categories have been considered like for ERP software, attributes such as manufacturing solution, supply chain solution and database solution. The above compilation may not be all inclusive and some people might choose to differ with it but it is almost near to perfect list.

CHAPTER EIGHT

Accounting Data Organization

Organizing and storing accounting data

To organize the accounting data properly, data should be rightly obtained and should be properly formatted and from the right resources. Once data is obtained next step is to process this data which is called as Data processing. Lets discuss data processing in detail.

Data processing:

Data processing is any computer process that converts data into information or knowledge. The processing is usually assumed to be automated and running on a computer. Because data are most useful when well-presented and actually informative, data-processing systems are often referred to as information systems to emphasize their practicality. Nevertheless, both terms are roughly synonymous, performing similar conversions; data-processing systems typically manipulate raw data into information, and likewise information systems typically take raw data as input to produce information as output.

To better market their profession, a computer programmer or a systems analyst that might once have referred, such as during the 1970s, to the computer systems that they produce as data- processing systems more often than not nowadays refers to the computer systems that they produce by some other term that includes the word information, such as information systems, information technology systems, or management information systems.

In the context of data processing, data are defined as numbers or characters that represent measurements from observable phenomena. A single datum is a single measurement from observable phenomena. Measured information is then algorithmically derived and/or logically deduced and/or statistically calculated from multiple data. (evidence). Information is defined as either a meaningful answer to a query or a meaningful stimulus that can cascade into further queries.

More generally, the term data processing can apply to any process that converts data from one format to another, although data conversion would be the more logical and correct term. From this perspective, data processing becomes the process of converting information into data and also the converting of data back into information. The distinction is that conversion doesn't require a question (query) to be answered. For example, information in the form of a string of characters forming a sentence in English is converted or encoded from a keyboard's key-presses as represented by hardware-oriented codes into ASCII codes after which it may be more easily processed by a computer—not as merely raw, amorphous data, but as a meaningful character in a natural language's set of graphemes—and finally converted or decoded to be displayed as characters, represented by a font on the computer display. In that example we can see the stage-by-stage conversion of the presence of and then absence of electrical conductivity in the key- press and subsequent release at the keyboard from raw substantially-meaningless hardware- oriented data to evermore-meaningful information as the processing proceeds toward the human being.

Techniques of Storage of Data:

For storing the accounting data, one may use the following techniques:

Two pass verification, also called double data entry, is a data entry quality control method that was originally employed when data records were entered onto sequential 80 column Hollerith cards with a keypunch. In the first pass through a set of records, the data keystrokes were entered onto each card as the data entry operator typed them. On the second pass through the batch, an operator at a separate machine, called a verifier, entered the same data. The verifier compared the second operator's keystrokes with the contents of the original card. If there were none, a verification notch was punched on the right edge of the card.

The later IBM 129 keypunch also could operate as a verifier. In that mode, it read a completed card (record) and loaded the 80 keystrokes into a buffer. A data entry operator reentered the record and the keypunch compared the new keystrokes with those loaded into the buffer. If a discrepancy occurred the operator was given a chance to reenter that keystroke and ultimately overwrite the entry in the buffer. If all keystrokes matched the original card, it was passed through and received a verification punch. If corrections were required then the operator was prompted to discard the original card and insert a fresh card on which corrected keystrokes were typed. The corrected record (card) was passed through and received a corrected verification punch.

Modern use:

While this method of quality control clearly is not proof against systematic errors or operator misread entries from a source document, it is very useful in catching and correcting random miskeyed strokes which occur even with experienced data entry operators. This method has survived the keypunch and is available in some currently available data entry programs (e.g. SPSS Data Entry for Windows). At least one study suggests that single pass data entry with range checks and skip rules approaches the reliability of two-pass data entry (see Controlled Clinical Trials from sometime in the 1990s - however it is desirable to implement both systems in a data entry application.

Capitalizing the Data Warehouse:

An asset is something that will have value in future periods, and the data warehouse (if it is any good) certainly fits into that definition. Companies capitalize their enterprise resource planning (ERP) systems and the guys with the green eyeshades don't object. Why not do the same for the data warehouse? A number of us have long maintained that the data warehouse (DW) is a real asset that has significant value to an organization -- some of us even believe that the DW will make the difference between a company living and dying. Because the DW provides value in future periods, it represents an intangible asset that should be capitalized on a company's balance sheet along with the tangible assets of cash, accounts receivable, inventory plant and machinery.

Current and Future Accounting Rules:

The current financial accounting rules are heavily criticized as not reflecting the true value of IT assets such as those of the ERP systems and data warehouses. Under the current rules of the Financial Accounting Standards number 141 and 142, a data warehouse, as an intangible asset, could be capitalized at its fair value only when a company with an internally built data warehouse is acquired by another corporation. Thus, the CIO would be rewarded for managing a high value asset only when the data warehouse has been purchased.

Today, a company with an internally created data warehouse would be shown as an intangible asset only at its capitalized historical cost. This historical cost probably does not capture the fair value of the completed project, nor does it capture all the costs associated with the data warehouse. The current accounting system in the United States allows one company to show a high value on the data warehouse that was purchased and a second company to have a lower value on a data warehouse that was internally developed. Thus, the company is not able to reflect the fair value created by the successful implementation of an internally developed data warehouse.

The *Financial Accounting Standards Board (FASB)* is working on a new standard to address the comparability issue between companies that have purchased data warehouses and companies that have built a data warehouse internally. The first step is a proposal to disclose in the footnotes of the financial statements the quantitative value of the substantially built up intangibles in a business. The eventual goal is to book the intangible assets at their fair value to allow the financial statements of different entities to be comparable and, to address our interests, for companies to accurately reflect the asset value of a data warehouse.

The FASB is also integrating the U.S. accounting rules to the International Accounting Standards (IAS). More than 90 countries have moved to the IAS standards in the past year, including all of Europe. The IAS standard No. 39 requires the company to currently book the data warehouse at the fair value of the assets, and now the data warehouse must be carried on the company's books. In most situations, this rewards management for successful efforts in creating and maintaining a data warehouse.

What Did the DW Cost?

The expenses for any DW will vary widely. The cost will be dependent on the size of the database, the number of users, the complexity and quality of the source data, the software tools employed, the need for consultants and contractors, the capabilities of the team, and how well the system is supported and maintained.

It's necessary to understand how costs will be accounted for. Some costs will be expensed immediately and others amortized over the expected life of the system. Costs will appear in different accounts, and all these factors will become important when the actual total costs are tabulated and the DW is capitalized.

The ***accounting approach*** to classifying the costs as current expenses or capitalized as assets is a three characteristic definition. If the associated costs fail any of the characteristics, then the cost should be expensed under current accounting rules. The first characteristic is future benefits. The future benefits are defined as the capacity, singly or in combination with other assets, to contribute directly or indirectly to future net cash inflows. The second characteristic is whether the enterprise has control. Control is defined as the ability to both derive future benefits and to deny that ability to others. The third characteristic is that the cost accumulation is based on a past event or transaction that gives rise to the future benefit.

Hardware: For the data warehouse, you will need CPUs, disks, networks and workstations. Some vendors, such as *Teradata*, usually bundle the hardware along with the relational database management system (RDBMS), and the DW appliances bundle the hardware, operating system and RDBMS. If existing desktops and laptops are adequate to support end users, no additional costs should be charged; however, if upgrades or new machines are required, the additional costs should be assigned and depreciated over the expected life of the system. Three years is often used as the expected life, even though the system will probably last longer. The calculation is the cost to purchase or upgrade times the number of anticipated users. The cost of the hardware should always be capitalized.

Software: The data warehouse always needs an RDBMS. Most installations employ end-user access and analysis tools such as *BusinessObjects, Cognos and MicroStrategy*. Many installations choose an extract, transform and load

(ETL) tool such as *Informatica* or DataStage rather than writing their own ETL code. Add-ons with the ETL tools could include additional costs for each different type of source file or target database. These tools are often priced based on the operating system and size of the machine. Additional tools are often needed for data cleansing and performance monitoring. Initial software costs should always be capitalized.

Internal Staff: The fully burdened rate (salary plus taxes, benefits, support costs, etc.) for the IT folks associated with the project should be included in the project cost. Business personnel are usually not included in calculations for personnel costs, but any help desk staff in the business organization should be. Include the fully burdened costs of the people on your project and capitalize these costs.

Consultants and Contractors: Consultants are engaged to help determine requirements, help plan the project, and create the scope agreement, cost justify the project, help select the software, and establish the initial and long-term architectures. Consultants are typically more expensive than contractors but usually don't remain on projects as long. Contractors are brought in to supplement technical skills, specifically for software such as the database management system (DBMS). The cost for contractors will be dependent on how deficient the organization is in the required skills, how fast the organization needs the system implemented and how long it will take to transfer skills once the implementation is complete. The costs of the consultants and contractors for the initial implementation and for any major enhancements (not maintenance) should be capitalized.

Training: You could make a case for the value of training, the intellectual capital, the knowledge and the increased capability of those who went through the training becoming an asset that would have value in future periods; however, because of employee turnover and other factors, accountants are reticent to claim the value of training as an asset. Training costs should be expensed as they are incurred and should not be capitalized.

Training fails the control test for being a capitalized asset. There are past expenditures for training and probable future benefits, but without enforceable work contracts, there is no entity control of specifically trained labor.

Operations and System Administration: This is a grab bag of roles and costs including monitoring the system performance, executing backups, administering security, administering the Meta data repository, dealing with the vendors and assigning charge-backs. The initial costs for operations and systems administration should be capitalized. The ongoing costs of both operations and system administration should not be capitalized unless there are major enhancements (because this represents day-to-day operations and not probable future benefits).

Data Quality Improvements: Every data warehouse implementation demands improvements in the quality of the data. The source files far too often contain data elements that are outside the valid values, data that is missing, incorrect data types and data that violate business rules (i.e., men getting hysterectomies, date of birth in the 22nd century, non-unique values for primary keys and incorrect data types). Most of this data must be cleansed before it's loaded into the data warehouse. Software is available to profile the data, which would provide information on most aspects of the quality of the data, and some software is specific to cleaning up names and addresses. Customer relationship management (CRM) data could now be de-duplicated, names and addresses would be corrected, deceased customers would be deleted and customers would have activity codes that are more correct. This is an expensive process, but the result is data that is much more valuable to the organization. The value comes from fewer wasted mailings, fewer customer interactions that cannot result in sales, more customized and more appropriate marketing, and a much better image of the organization to the customer. The improvements in data quality should result in more sales, more cross-selling, greater profitability per customer interaction, and lower mailing and printing costs. For the DW, the improvements in data quality will mean far less checking and rechecking of results. The improved data quality will mean that the organization's strategic and tactical decisions will be supported by better information, and those making the decisions will be more likely to take action on results they trust. The value of the improved CRM data will be realized in future periods and should therefore be considered as an asset, and the following costs should be capitalized: data quality software purchase, consulting and internal personnel costs.

Meta Data: Capturing and maintaining Meta data is an expensive effort, but it is generally recognized as a critical success factor for a data warehouse. Business meta data should include data definitions, domains (valid values), business rules, uniqueness, data source, security, timeliness and the owner of the data. Some meta data can be generated automatically from the modeling tools, the ETL tools and the BI tools; however, architecting how the meta data will be captured and maintained is not simple. It will require smart internal people or perhaps consulting help. In addition, an organization may choose to purchase Meta data products. Meta data will be valuable to analysts, report developers and report recipients because the Meta data will reduce their efforts to research and gather the data. It will also be valuable in giving them a better understanding of the results. *CRM* meta data capture codes would indicate a customer's value, previous purchases (retailing) and average balances (banking). *CRM* for law enforcement would have codes for a person's violence level, an insurance company would have codes representing the likelihood of a customer discontinuing paying their premiums. Meta data will have value in future periods (as long as it's properly maintained) and should therefore be considered an asset, and the following costs should be capitalized: meta data software purchase, consulting and internal personnel costs.

Data Modeling: The effort to develop the data models to support the DW should be capitalized, but not the ongoing maintenance of the models.

Performance and Availability: Supporting the service level agreements (SLAs) for performance and availability will require new processes and procedures, possibly new monitoring software, possibly more hardware, and possibly some consulting and contracting effort. The costs for this area should be capitalized, but not any ongoing maintenance.

The Life cycle of Data:

So how can we determine when data needs to be archived? In order to accurately answer that question we need to understand the different states of data as it progresses through its lifespan.

There is delineation in various states of data over its useful life. Data is created at some point, usually by means of a transaction: a product is released, an order is processed, a deposit is made, etc. For a period of time after creation, the data enters it first state: it is operational. That is, the data is needed to complete on-going business transactions. This is where it serves it primary business purpose. Transactions are enacted upon data in this state.

The operational state is followed by the reference state. This is the time during which the data is still needed for reporting and query purposes. It could be to produce internal reports, external statements, or simply exist in case a customer asks for it.

Then, after some additional period of time, the data moves into an area where it is no longer needed for completing business transactions and the chance of it being needed for querying and reporting is small to none. However, the data still needs to be saved for regulatory compliance and other legal purposes, particularly if it pertains to a financial transaction. This is the archive state. It is the requirements for data in this state which this white paper addresses.

Finally, after a designated period of time in the archive, the data is no longer needed at all and it can be discarded. This actually should be emphasized much stronger: the data must be discarded. In most cases the only reason older data is being kept at all is to comply with regulations, many of which help to enable lawsuits. When there is no legal requirement to maintain such data, it is only right and proper for organizations to demand that it be destroyed - why enable anyone to sue you if it is not a legal requirement to do so?

Don't think in terms of databases or technologies that you already know when considering these data states. The data could be in three separate databases, a single database, or any combination thereof. Furthermore, don't think about data warehousing in this context - here we are talking about the single, official store of data - and its production lifecycle.

From here-on out we will use the terms introduced here for the various states of data throughout its lifecycle, with the emphasis being on archiving database data and the issues arising from doing so.

CHAPTER NINE

Database Archiving

What is Database Archiving?

Database Archiving is part of a larger topic, namely Data Archiving. Data exists in many formats and for many purposes, and only a small percentage of it is actually in a database. Physical documents, electronic documents, computer files and data sets, e-mail, and multimedia files are all examples of data that may reasonably need to be archived at some point. Refer to Figure 2. Each of these "things" needs to be archived to fulfill regulatory, legal, and business requirements.

But each type of data requires different archival processing requirements due to its form and nature. What works to archive e-mail is not sufficient for archiving database data, and so on. In other words, type of data may need to command its own technology. This is most certainly true for database data. Why?

Well, data stored in a database is different than other types of data in many ways. The main advantage of using a DBMS is to impose a logical, structured organization on the data. A *DBMS* provides a layer of independence between the data and the applications that use the data. In other words, applications are insulated from how data is structured and stored. The interface to the data is through the DBMS data language, whether it is SQL for relational databases, DL/1 for IMS, or even *XQuery* for XML databases. So the archival of data from a database requires knowledge of, and operation in conjunction with, the mechanisms and interfaces of the DBMS.

If we now accept that database archiving is a subset of data archiving, let's define exactly what we mean by the term. Database Archiving is the process of removing selected data records from operational databases that are not expected to be referenced again and storing them in an archive data store where they can be retrieved if needed.

Let's examine each of the major components of that last sentence. We say removing because the data is deleted from the operational database when it is moved to the data archive. Recall our earlier discussion of the data lifecycle. When data moves into the archive state, query and access is no longer anticipated to be required.

Next, we say selected records. This is important because we do not want to archive database data at the file level. We need only those specific pieces of data that are no longer needed for operational and reference purposes by the business. This means that the archive needs to be able to selectively choose particular pieces of related data for archival... not the whole database, not an entire table or segment, and not even a specific row. Instead, all of the data that represents a business object is archived at the same time. For example, if we choose to archive order data, we would also want to archive the specifics about each item on that order. This data likely spans multiple constructs within the database (tables for DB2 or Oracle; segments and/or databases for IMS).

The next interesting piece of the definition is this: and storing them (the data) in an archive data store. This implies that the data is stored separately from the operational database and does not require either the DBMS or the operational applications any longer. Archived data is separate and independent from the production systems from which it was moved.

The final component of the definition that warrants clarification is... where they can be retrieved if needed. The whole purpose of archiving is to maintain the data in case it is required for some purpose. The purpose may be external, in the form of a lawsuit or to support a governmental regulation; or the purpose may be internal, in the form of a new business practice or requirement. At any rate, the data needs to be readily accessible in a reasonable timeframe without requiring a lot of manual manipulation. I mean, let's face it, anyone can archive data if they don't have to worry about how to query it later, right?

Functions of Accounting:

- Traditional Views:
    - Record, Classify, Summaries & Interpret data affecting the organization's finances.
    - Provide information useful for decision making

- Contemporary View:
- A system for capturing and storing an organization's data in one integrated repository.

The Role of Accountant:

- which events to capture data about,
- what data relating to each event should be captured,
- how that data is to be captured while preventing input errors,
- how the data should be stored to optimize its usability while maintaining its integrity,
- how meaningful reports can be generated on demand in real-time.

Problems with the Traditional View:

- "transactions" orientation as opposed to an "events" orientation:

Events are very important. In fact, most interaction of users with the accounting system is via events.

- narrow focus on financial data,

Non-financial information is crucial for decision-making. Accounting system needs to be integrated with the overall information system of the organization.

- reporting is periodic and not real-time,

Often, managers and other users need accounting information in real-time for decision- making.

- limited accessibility of information,

Accessibility to accounting information should be on "need-to-know" basis.

- too high a level of aggregation, information should be provided at levels of aggregation appropriate to the decisions.
- limited flexibility which prevents answering queries that cross functional boundaries.,

    - *adaptable to changes in operations*
    - *adaptable to changes in technology*

Traditional Computerized Accounting Systems: File-Oriented Systems:

- Each application owns its own data -- duplication/ redundancies in data.
- Lack of uniformity of meaning of data -- not possible for accounting applications to share data.
- Difficult to enforce uniform standards ---lack of integrity of data.
- Difficulties in accessing data -- need to know programs to access data.

Designing simple accounting vouchers:

Accounting Vouchers may be classified into following six types:

1. **Payment** : For recording payment made to any party by cash or cheque. If the payment is made to the supplier then the voucher is prepared semi-automatically using command Make Payment to Supplier .
2. **Receipt** : For recording receipts from any party by cash or cheque. If the payment is received from the customer then the voucher is prepared semi automatically using command Receive Payment from customer .
3. **Journal** : Voucher where neither account head is cash or cheque can be called journal voucher.
4. **Contra** : To cater to concept of contra entries and for treatment of cheques received and issued by the business.
5. **Sales** : For regarding sales voucher means any product sale by supplier to customer or any dealing between cash or cheque .
6. **Purchase** : For regarding purchase voucher means any product purchase by customer to supplier or any dealing between cash or cheque.

In fact the different voucher types help in classifying the different types of transactions and they do no affect the way the voucher is posted in the ledger.

All Standard Accounting Vouchers - with support for User Defined Vouchers.

Tally works the way accountants do. It's comprehensive accounting and inventory control capabilities allow you to enter all types of transactions that you require to conduct your business efficiently.

Vouchers types like Payments, Receipts, Sales, Purchases, Journals, Debit & Credit Notes, Delivery Challans, Goods Inward Notes, Stock Journals, Physical Stock Vouchers, Contras & Memos, Sales & Purchase Orders and Rejection Notes are available.

Tally also allows for a flexible Voucher Numbering System. You can select between Automatic or Manual numbering of Vouchers (including Multiple Series).

In addition, you can also create your own voucher types like "Citibank Payment Voucher" or "Export Sales Invoice" . With the powerful 'Voucher Class' facility you can can pre-configure each voucher type to accept only that ledgers that you specify - thereby eliminating data entry errors.

Extracting desired accounting information from sources:

To extract the desired accounting information, accounting system need to interact with different sub systems of the organization like Invoicing sytem, BOM, Sales and marketing system, payroll system, HR management systems. All these systems use the modern database approach than traditional file based system. Lets discuss the database approach to accounting system in detail.

Advantages of the database approach:

- supports the capturing of financial and non-financial data
- support for real-time rather than periodic reporting
- better controlled accessibility of data
- storage of data in the most disaggregated form

- Uniformity of meaning of data -- supported by a rigorous data model
- Enforcement of access controls easier

CHAPTER TEN

Accounting Fundamentals and Generating of Reports

To Understand the computerized accounting, one need to understand all the basic fundamentals of accounting which include accounting ledger, cash book, bank book , trial balance, Profit and loss accounts and their adjustments, balance sheet and accounting related reports. Let's discuss these in detail:

Accounting Ledger:

Ledger is the most important book of accounting. It contains summarized, classified description of all the business transactions. It is divided into various parts and each part is termed as 'account'. It is necessary to gather at one place all transactions, during the period, relating to a particular subject-a person, a thing, a class of expenses, incomes etc. It is only then that the net results can be ascertained.

Thus the first step in the procedure of recording transactions is to journalize and the second step is to post the transactions in the ledger. Ledger is known as the 'principal or chief'. book of accounts. In ledger the financial information is classified by its nature and relevance.

The statement which records the transactions at one place relating to a particular subject is known as account. The book which contains all the accounts is known as ledger and the procedure of writing up the accounts is known as posting.

The ledger is the most important book of account and is the destination of the entries made in the Journal or Sub-divided Journals. It is a collection of all the three types of accounts --Personal, Real and Nominal. If you are faced with questions like:

- How much a particular customer owes you?
- What is the amount payable by you to anyone of your suppliers?
- What is the amount of goods purchased by you during specific period ?
- How much sales you have affected during, say, last three months?
- What has been your expenditure on, say, labor during the period?

Then the quicker and easier way of ascertaining the relevant information is to turn to your ledger, find out the balance of the Customer's A/c or Supplier's A/c or Purchases A/c or Sales A/c or Wages A/c.

How to write Ledger

In ledger we maintain accounts. Each account is allotted one or more pages depending upon the requirement. Ledger is usually ruled in anyone of the following two alternatives. First alternative is followed in those cases where balance is required to be ascertained after every transaction e.g. Banks.

Second alternative is followed in those cases where balance is required to be ascertained only periodically, say after a month or quarterly. In your study of book-keeping and accountancy T- shape accounts will be used (alternative-two).

The transactions are entered in the ledger accounts in order of dates. Every entry must be dated which must be shown in the column meant for date. This is the first column on the left of each side of the account.

Record the relevant amount on the left-hand side of the account which, according to the journal is to be debited and record the amount on the right-hand side of the account which, as per journal, is to be credited (use 'amount columns' for this purpose). In ledger account each entry on the debit (left-hand) side commences with the word "To" and one the credit (right- hand) side with the word "By". In the 'particulars column' reference is made to the other account involved for providing cross reference. In the 'folio column' would be entered the page of the journal (or page of the relevant sub-divided journal) from which entry has been posted and in the folio column of journal, the page number of the ledger is written on which the relevant account appears.

Following the above procedure of recording the entries in the ledger will in fact amount to this The account receiving the benefit in shape of cash or goods will receive the debits and the account imparting i.e. giving away the benefit will receive the credits.

Balancing the Accounts

Whenever it is desired to balance an account, the two sides are added up, and if the totals of the two sides are unequal then the difference is put on the side having lesser total. This will make both the sides equal. The amount of the difference inserted is known as 'balance' of the account. In particulars column it is written as Balance c/d (carried down). In subsequent period it is known as Balance bid (brought down). If the total of the credit side of the account is less, the balance will be inserted on credit side with the words "By Balance c/d". This balance is known as Debit Balance and after closing the account it will be shown on the debit side with the words "To Balance bid". Similarly if the total of debit side of the account is less, the balance will be inserted on debit side with the words "To Balance c/d". This balance is known as Credit Balance and after closing the account it will be shown on the credit side with the words "By Balance bid".

Personal Accounts

It is worthwhile to refresh your memory and recall that personal accounts relate to individuals and business entities (firm; company, corporation etc.) and the rule is : Receiver is to be debited and giver is to be credited. Now if on any particular date the business wants to know as to how much amount is 'due to' or 'due by' a particular person to itself (business) then it should balance the account of the person concerned. Debit balance as per personal account signifies that the person is the debtor of the business i.e.

person owes an amount equal to the balance to the business or the amount, represented by the balance is 'due to' the business by the person. Similarly, Credit balance as per personal account signifies that the person is the creditor of the business i.e. business owes an amount equal to the balance to the person or the amount represented by the balance is 'due by' the business to the person.

Real Account

These are the accounts relating to property or possession or rights. Rule is : "What comes in is to be debited and what goes out is to be credited." Thus all incomings are to be recorded on the debit side and outgoings on the credit side. On any particular date these accounts should have 'debits balance' representing the worth of the item covered by the account. At the end of the year (generally) or at any other point of time when the financial position of the business is required to be ascertained these accounts are balanced. These balances are shown on the assets side of the statement of position or Balance Sheet. These accounts do have 'debit balance' which signifies the 'book-value' or 'written down value' or 'going concern-value' of the assets of the business as on that relevant date.

Nominal Accounts

These are the accounts showing the various heads of expenses and sources of income. At the end of the specified period (generally one year) these accounts are closed by transfer to the final accounts i.e. Trading or Profit and Loss Account.

Necessity of Ledger:

Maintaining of ledger is a must in every accounting system. It is necessary as will be clear from its advantages:

1. Transactions relating to a particular person, item or heading of expenditure‘ or income are grouped in the concerned account at one place.
2. When each account is periodically balanced it reflects the net position of that account. For example, how much is due from a customer or how much is payable to a supplier or what is the value of total purchases or what has been the expenditure on salaries? Such information is available by balancing the ledger accounts.
3. Ledger is the stepping stone for preparing Trial Balance- which tests the arithmetical accuracy' .of the accounting books. .
4. Since the entries recorded in the journal are referenced into ledger the possibility of errors or defalcations are reduced to the minimum.
5. Ledger is the destination of all entries made in journal or sub-journals.
6. Ledger is the "store-house" of all information which subsequently is used for preparing final accounts and financial statements.

Opening entry and its posting. In the case of an existing business we are required to pass an entry in the journal (on the basis of the Balance Sheet prepared at the end of the previous year) for bringing in the new books all assets and liabilities: this is known as Opening entry.

Differences between Journal and Ledger.

Journal:

1. Is the book of prime entry.
2. As soon as transaction originates it is recorded in journal
3. Transactions are recorded in order of occurrence i.e. strictly in order of dates.
4. Narration (brief description) is written for each entry.
5. Ledger folio is written
6. Relevant information cannot be ascertained readily e.g. cash in hand can't be found out easily.
7. Final accounts can't be prepared directly from journal.
8. Accuracy of the books can't be tested.
9. Debit and credit amounts of a transaction are recorded in adjacent columns.
10. Journal has two columns one for debit amount another for credit amount.
11. Journal is not balanced.
12. With the computerization of accounting journal may not be used for routine transactions like receipts, purchases, sales etc

Ledger:

1. Is the book of final entry.
2. Transactions are posted in the ledger after the same have been recorded in the journal.

3. Transactions are classified according to the nature and are grouped in the concerned accounts.
4. Narration is not required.
5. Folio of the journal or sub-journal is written.
6. Since transactions of particular nature are grouped at one place therefore relevant information can be ascertained.
7. Ledger is the basis of preparing final accounts.
8. Accuracy of the books is tested by means of list of balances.
9. Debit and credit amounts of a transaction are recorded in two different sides of two different accounts.
10. Ledger has two sides: left side is debit side right side is credit side.
11. Every account in the ledger is balanced at appropriate time.
12. Ledger cannot be avoided. However it may be loose leaf ledger or a computerized ledger. But ledger is a must

Accounting Sub Journals - Cash Book:

The accounting procedure, for recording information, involves two steps, namely journalizing and posting. It follows that every business must maintain a journal (books of original or prime entry) and a ledger (principal book). Thus the system of book-keeping originally envisages that all the transactions must be recorded first in the book of original record, i.e., journal and then each transaction so recorded in the journal should be posted in the principal book, i.e., ledger. Subsequently it was experienced that the labor of recording each transaction with narration in the journal and then posting each entry in two different accounts in the ledger was enormous. The procedure was more time-consuming and resulted in higher establishment cost.

It is but natural that in every business most of the transactions relate to receipts and payments of cash; purchases of goods ;. sales of goods etc. It was found to be convenient and economical to keep separate books to record each particular class of transactions. Each separate book meant to record transactions of a particular class is the book of original or prime entry. It is also known as sub-journal or subsidiary book. The system under which transactions of similar nature are entered in the relevant' subsidiary book and on the basis of which ledger is written is known as the 'practical system of book- keeping'. This system reduces labor and time of recording the transactions as impersonal accounts, viz., sales account, purchases account etc., receive the

posting of totals and not of individual transactions. However, this system also conforms to the basic rules of the double entry system.

Generally the following subsidiary books are used in the business:

i. ***Cash book*** : records receipts and payments of cash including transactions relating to bank.
ii. ***Purchases book***: records credit purchases of goods meant for sale or for conversion into finished goods.
iii. ***Returns outwards book***: records return of the goods to the suppliers due to several reasons.
iv. ***Sales book***: records credit sales of the goods dealt in by the business;

v. ***Returns inwards book***: records the return of goods by the customers to the business.
vi. ***Bills receivable book***: records the receipts of bills of exchange, promissory notes and hundies of various parties.
vii. ***Bills payable book***: records the issue of bills exchange, promissory notes and hundies to the various parties.

Advantages of sub-journals:

i. It results in saving of time by (a) enabling the recording procedure to be carried on simultaneously in different subsidiary books and (b) by posting the periodical totals in the impersonal accounts.
ii. It makes information available regarding each particular class of transactions.
iii. At the time of preparing trial balance the checking is easier because books being many, different persons can carry out the job.

Cash Book:

In any business, perhaps, the largest number of transactions of one nature must relate to cash and bank. It is so because every transaction must, ultimately, result in a cash transaction. Now if every cash transaction is to be recorded in journal, it will involve an enormous amount of labor in debiting or crediting cash or bank account in the ledger for each transaction. Therefore, it is convenient to have a separate book, the cash book, to record such transactions. Maintaining of cash book removes the necessity of having cash and bank accounts in the ledger. This book enables us to know the balance of cash in hand and at bank at any point of time.

Cash book consists of cash and bank accounts taken out of ledger and maintained separately; thus it is a substitute of ledger for cash and bank accounts. It is also a book of original entry because cash and bank transactions are not recorded in any other subsidiary book.

Types of cash book:

The type of cash book to be used by any business will depend upon its nature and requirements. It may be anyone of the following:

a. Single column cash book (cash column).
b. Double column cash book (cash and discount columns).
c. Triple column cash book (cash, discount and bank columns).
d. Bank cash book (bank and discount columns).

Generally, each business will use anyone of the above types of cash book along with "petty cashbook" which is maintained on memorandum basis.

Distinction between cash A/c and Cash book:

Actually cash book is a perfect substitute of cash account. In both, cash transactions are recorded date wise in order of occurrence. Cash balance as on any date can be ascertained by balancing both on any day desired. Yet there are some differences between the two as given below:

Cash account:

1. Is an account in the ledger.
2. Cash account is part of the ledger. Cash account is opened in the ledger in which posting is done from some book of original entry i.e. journal
3. In cash account posting is not followed by narration.
4. It only records one aspect of transaction involving cash and bank.

Cash book:

1. Is a separate book of accounts forming part of accounting system.
2. Cash book records entries directly from transactions and these is no need for a book of prime entry.
3. In cash book entries are followed by narration also.
4. It records both the aspects of this transaction in cash and bank columns to complete double entry posting.

Single Column Cash Book:

It has only one. column on each side for amount In fact, it is written just like cash account in the ledger (being real account what comes in is debited; what goes out is credited). This form of 'cash book has the same ruling as that of a ledger account There is no need of having a cash account in the ledger. The purpose is ably served by cash book itself. Posting from debit (receipt) side of the cash book is done to the credit side of concerned accounts and from the credit side of cash book to the debit side of concerned accounts.

Balancing:

The cash book is balanced in the same manner as a ledger account. As more cash cannot be paid then what we have, therefore the cash balance (if any) must always be a debit balance. Therefore, the receipts column will always be bigger than the payments column. The difference will be written on the credit side as "By balance c/d". The totals are then entered in the two columns opposite one another and then on the debit side the balance is written as *"To balance b/d"*. It shows the cash balance in hand in the beginning of the next period. To verify the accuracy of the entries made, the cash book should be balanced frequently (preferably daily). The balance as per cash book must tally with the actual cash in hand.

Double Column Cash Book:

As the phenomenon of offering and accepting cash discount is intimately associated with the act of receipt and payment of cash, therefore, the utility of cash book increases if the columns of discount are also provided in it. Cash book having additional columns for discount is known as double column cash book.

Triple Column Cash Book:

These days it is difficult to carryon any business without having dealings with the bank. Normally bulk of its funds is kept by the business at a bank in a current account where frequent withdrawals and deposits are permitted. Bank transactions, i.e.. payments into and out of bank are more numerous than cash transactions. Therefore, it is appropriate as well as convenient that cash book should have one additional column on each side to record moneys deposited at bank arid payments out of the hank. The additional advantage to having this type of cash book is that bank account is not required to be maintained in the ledger.

Before we explain the method of writing up the triple column cash book you should be familiar with the concept of 'contra entries'. Also note carefully the treatment of cheques received and issued by the business.

Contra Entries:

In the three column cash book there will be some cross or contra entries i.e.. transfer of money from cash to bank (amount deposited) and vice versa (amount withdrawn from bank for office use). In all such cases both entries occur in the cash book and no ledger entry is required. This is indicated by a contra sign (C) in the folio column indicating thereby that the double entry aspect of this transaction is complete and it requires no posting to the ledger. Treatment of cheques in a triple-column cash book is explained below:

1. Cheques received and deposited in the bank on the same day: When the cheques received from the debtors are deposited in the bank on the day of receipt itself the entry is recorded in the bank column on the debit side of the cash book therefrom debtor's account receives credit.
2. Cheques received but deposited in the bank on a later date: At the time when cheque is received it is recorded in the cash column on the debit side of the cash book and the date on which it is deposited in the bank, Two steps are required:-

i. Enter the same in the cash column on the credit side of the cash book "By Bank A/c" and
ii. Enter it in the bank column on the debit side of the cash book' 'To Cash A/c". Thus it assumes the form of Contra entry on the day of depositing the cheque into bank received earlier.

However, if there is no information as to the date of deposit of the cheque, it should beassumed that the cheque was deposited in the bank on the date of receipt.

3. Cheques received and endorsed in favor of some creditor :- On receipt, cheque is recorded in the cash column on the debit side and at the time of endorsement the same is recorded in cash column on credit side, By Creditors Ale.
4. Bearer cheques may be en cashed at the counter of the bank or it may be deposited in the bank. In case it is encashed it should be recorded in the cash column on the debit side, in case it is deposited in the bank the same should be recorded in the bank column on the

debit side of the cash book.

Cash book is a Journalized ledger:

Often a question is asked whether cash book is a journal or ledger? It is journal in the sense that all cash transactions are primarily recorded in the cash book with narration and therefore, these are posted to the relevant accounts in the ledger. Cash book is also ledger in the sense that it serves the purpose of cash account and bank account (in case of triple column cash book). No separate cash account is opened in the ledger where cash book is in existence. Thus cash book is a unique combination of journal and ledger. It is popularly known as journalized ledger.

Similarities of Cash book with journal:

1. Cash transactions are recorded in the cash book at the time of origin i.e. primary book.
2. Transactions are recorded date-wise.
3. Transactions from cash book posted to the relevant accounts (except cash account) in the ledger.
4. Cash book contains ledger folio as in the journal.
5. Narration is given for each entry.

Similarities of Cash book with ledger:

1. Form of cash book resembles with ledger. Two sides left hand side is the debit side (receipts) Right hand side is

the credit side (payments).

2. Words "To" and "By" are used as in the ledger.
3. No separate cash account and bank account are required in the ledger. Thus cash book is the book of final entry entry for cash and bank transactions.
4. Cash and bank columns of the cash book are periodically, balanced just like ledger accounts.

Maintaining cash Book, Posting and Balancing:

In the case of a new business the amount will be written in the cash column if the cash is introduced and in the bank column if it is directly deposited in the bank with the words, "To Capital Account "on the debit-side of the cash book. In the case of a continuing business the opening balances are written as "To Balance b/d"

Receipt side of the cash book. (Dr. Side):

It is used to record all receipts both in cash and by cheques as also to record the discount allowed to our debtors while receiving the payment. Cash receipts are entered in the cash column whereas amounts received by cheques are entered in the bank column; (It is always advisable to follow the practice of crossing all cheques received as "Payees Ale only" and to be sent to bank for collection. This provides safeguard against possible embezzlement) and discount allowed in the discount column.

Posting from the debit side of the cash book:

It is to the credit of the respective accounts-in case if personal account credit is to be given for cash or cheque received plus discount allowed. At periodical intervals cash and bank columns will be balanced and the balance will be carried down to the next period whereas discount column will be to totaled and posted to the debit side of "Discount Allowed" account to be maintained in the ledger. Payment side of the cash book (Cr. Side) is used to record all payments both in cash and through cheques as also to record the discount received or availed by us from our creditors while making payment to them. Cash payments are recorded in the cash column, payments through cheques are entered in the bank column and discount received in the discount column.

Posting from the credit side of the cash book:

It is to the debit of the respective account-in case of personal accounts debit is to be given for the total of the payments made and discount received. At periodical intervals the discount column will be totaled and posted to the credit of "Discount received account" in the ledger.

Balancing:

The cash columns are balanced exactly in the same manner as explained in the case of single column cash book. Discount columns are totaled but not balanced. Bank columns are also balanced just like cash columns. Since the banks allows overdraft therefore it is possible for, the business to withdraw more than the amount deposited. In such a case the total of the bank column on the credit side will be bigger than the one on the debit side. The difference is written on the debit side as "To Balance c/d"

Bank (Cash Book) A/c:

Whenever cash is being handled by the employees there is always danger that employees might embezzle cash. In order to minimize this risk many of the business units follow this policy:

i. All cash received is deposited in the bank intact i.e.. no part of the cash received is used for meeting day-to- day .payments ;
ii. All cheques received are also sent to the bank for collection; (iil) All payments are to be made by the issue of cheques.

However small payments like carriage, postage, local conveyance etc., which. by nature, cannot be, paid by cheque should be dealt through another cash book known as "Petty Cash Book". We will discuss it later in this very chapter.

If the above scheme is adopted, then there is hardly any chance that the employee receiving the cash can misappropriate cash either temporarily or permanently. The only care you should exercise is to see whether the daily total of receipts tallies with the amount deposited in the bank (either on the same day or on the next working day) or not.

This can be verified from the counterfoil of the ‘pay-in-slip’. If you decide to make use of this type of .cash book for your business then it should have only two columns on each side, Bank &Discount. There is no need to have cash column. It may also be called as "Cash book without cash column" or "Bank cash book".

How to write up? All receipts, whether in cash or by cheque should be entered on the debit side of the book in bank column. All payments to be entered on the credit side of the book in bank column. Treatment of discount allowed and discount received' is the same as discussed earlier.

Posting is also similar to as described under triple column cash book.

Subsidiary Accounting Books:

Subsidiary books or sub-journals or special journals are the various names used to describe practical system of book keeping. As the size of business grew the volume of transactions of all the business houses rose alarmingly and it was realized that journal was inadequate as the only book of original entry. It was found to be convenient and advantageous to have different books of original entries for different activities of the business like purchases, sales, purchases returns and sales returns etc.

Special journals:

These are the journals in which special classes of transactions are recorded such as ; Purchases book records purchases of goods on credit; Sales book records sales of godson credit; Purchases returns book records the return of goods purchased (returns outwards) ;Sales returns book records the return of goods sold (return inwards) ; Bills receivable book records the bills accepted by the debtors and Bills payable book records the bills drawn by the creditors.

General Journal:

Records those transactions which do not fall within the scope of special journals. Such transactions usually relate to

1. Opening entries
2. Closing entries
3. Transfer entries
4. Rectification entries
5. Adjusting entries
6. Credit purchase of assets
7. Credit sale of discarded or obsolete fixed assets etc.

Difference between General Journal and Special Journal General Journal.

1. Transactions for which no special journal exists are recorded.
2. Each transaction is posted to ledger separately.
3. Ruling of journal is identical.
4. Essential part of accounting process.

Special Journal:

1. Specific types of transactions are recorded in each special journal.
2. Only the periodical totals are posted in group a. counts like purchases or sales account.
3. Ruling is modified as the requirements of the business e.g., additional columns for excise duty or sales tax may be provided.
4. Optional as per the desire of the business.

Purchases Book:

Purchases Book is also known as 'Invoice Journal' or 'Bought Journal' or Purchases Journal, issued for recording credit purchases of goods meant for resale. Cash purchases will not be entered in Purchases Book (to be entered in cash book) and credit purchases of goods not meant for resale viz., assets shall be entered in journal proper and not in the purchases book.

Form of the Purchases Book: Usual Purchase book should have columns for date, invoice number, particulars, ledger folio, details and amount.

Invoice:

When we purchase goods on credit we receive a statement from the supplier giving the particulars of the goods supplied by him. This statement is called an invoice. The invoice states the quantity, price and value of goods supplied. It also states the discounts allowable (trade and cash) and the conditions under which payment is expected.

Trade Discount:

It is an allowance made by the supplier to the retailers off the catalogue or invoice or list price. (The object of allowing 'trade discount' is to enable the retailer to sell the goods to the consumer at list price and still leaving margin for meeting business expenses and his profit.) Trade discount is offered without reference to the time factor within which supplier expects to receive the payment. Entries in the books of both supplier as well as retailer are made on the basis of net amount i.e. invoice price less trade discount.

It may be distinguished from cash discount as follows:

Trade discount

1. It is a concession "off the catalogue price" and allowed on purchases.
2. It is not recorded in ledger accounts.
3. It is deducted from the invoice.

Cash discount

1. It is a concession allowed on payment being made "within certain period"
2. Ledger account is maintained for discount allowed and availed.
3. It is not deducted from the invoice.

Sales Book:

In this book are recorded all goods sold on credit. The ruling is similar to that of purchases book. If there are cash sales they are recorded in cash book and sale of assets (distinguish between goods and assets) are recorded in the journal proper. The entries in the sales book are made from the copies of the invoices which have been sent to the customers along with the .goods. Such copies of the invoices may be termed as *'Outward invoice'*. Each such outward invoice should be numbered consecutively and the reference be given in the sales book along with the entry..

Purchases Returns Book:

This book is also known as "Returns Outwards Book". It records all returns of goods bought. Goods purchased may have to be returned to the supplier for various reasons such as not up to sample or not ordered or damaged during the transit etc. The ruling of the return books is identical with the ruling of purchases book. Debit Note. While returning the goods to the suppliers a letter is sent to them for their information and stating therein that we have debited your account by this amount on account of goods being returned herewith for the reasons stated. Generally such "information letters' are printed with counterfoil. Debit notes are sent to the parties concerned the counterfoils providing the base for writing up the purchases returns book.

Credit Note:

When a debit note is received along with the goods returned from the customer, itis a claim on us. If claim is accepted then Credit Note, usually printed in red ink, with full details is sent to the customer signifying our acceptance of the goods and customer's account being given the required credit. Counterfoils provide the base for writing up the Sales Returns Book.

Sales Returns Book:

This book is also known as "Returns inwards book" . It records all returns of goods sold. Goods sold may be returned. by our customers for various reasons such as goods sent being of wrong description or inferior quality or damaged. Ruling is identical with the ruling of sales book. Credit Note: When a debit note is received along with the goods returned from the customer, it is a claim on us. If claim is accepted then Credit Note, usually printed in red ink, with full details is sent to the customer signifying our acceptance of the goods and customer's account being given the required credit. Counterfoils provide the base for writing up the Sales Returns Book.

Bills Receivable Book:

All receipts of bills are entered in a book called bills receivable book. Whenever a bill of exchange is received its particulars are entered in the appropriate columns of the Bills Receivable Book. Posting from bills receivable book- The periodical total of the bills receivable book is posted to the debit of the bills receivable account in the ledger. Each entry in the book is posted to the credit of the individual account from whom the bill is received.

Bills Payable Book:

The details of the bills accepted by a trader are recorded in the book known as Bills Payable Book. Posting of the bills payable book-The periodical total of the bills payable book is posted to the credit of the bills payable account in the ledger. Each entry in the book is posted to the debit of the individual account to whom the bill is granted.

Bank book:

Definition : It is defined as the pass book of the depositor, in which the receiving teller writes the separate deposits. The bookkeeper enters the paid checks at stated intervals

Bank Book allows you to transfer funds, apply bank charges, and other cash functions to keep your financial reports accurate and up-to-date.

For e.g : progression bank book is software for handling the bank book

Progression's Bank Book (B/B) module manages and reconciles all of your cash accounts, giving you information about your company's cash flow and empowering you to make more proactive decisions. Progression's B/B will also allow you to transfer cash between cash accounts and maintain cash accounts in multiple currencies when used in conjunction with Progression's Currency Manager (C/M) module.

Receiving Cash:

When your company receives cash, you have the option of entering it into the system in three ways: as a prepayment in Order Entry (O/E), directly against a customer account in Accounts Receivable (A/R), or as part of a deposit ticket in Bank Book. This flexibility enables Progression to take control of your cash receipts regardless of how your company receives its income.

Spending cash:

In addition to receiving cash, checks generated in Accounts Payable (A/P) and Payroll (PR) are recorded in B/B. This allows Progression's Bank Book to monitor all outgoing transactions facilitating cash management and account reconciliation. You also can enter bank transactions such as service charges and interest earned directly into Progression's Bank Book to ensure complete accuracy.

Cash management planning and reporting:

Progression's Bank Book allows you to monitor your company's cash position by report and online. Planned receipts and disbursements may be entered in the Cash Flow Transaction application, allowing you to plan transactions before they actually occur. This provides a more accurate interpretation of your future cash position.

Central access to cash balances:

You can view any cash account you have in Progression from within Progression's Bank Book. This inquiry displays reconciliation information, along with book value, bank value, currency code and bank information. With Progression's Bank Book package, you can streamline your cash management planning process to improve the efficiency and operation of your business.

Bank Book for Windows Overview:

Bank Book for Windows: gives you an easy way to gather and organize information about all your accounts. The Bank Book includes fields for transaction name, category, amount, comment, date. It allows an unlimited number of entries and automatically sorts them.

Benefits, Features:

- Notebook-like interface;
- Intuitive, easy-to-use, very fast, and small;
- Easily search for information;
- Define filters to display only selected records;
- Print reports from the program;
- Display summaries;

Requirements: PC 286 CPU or better; 2 MB RAM; Color monitor; Windows 95, 98, Me, or 3.1; Requires only 400 Kbytes of disk space

Trial Balance:

Trial balance: After all transactions have been posted from the journal to the ledger, it is a good practice to prepare a trial balance. A trial balance is simply a listing of the ledger accounts along with their respective debit or credit balances. The trial balance is not a formal financial statement, but rather a self-check to determine that debits equal credits.

Debits equal credits: Since each transaction was journalized in a way that insured that debits equaled credits, one would expect that this equality would be maintained throughout the ledger and trial balance. If the trial balance fails to balance, an error has occurred and must be located. It is much better to be careful as you go, rather than having to go back and locate an error after the fact. You should also be aware that a "balanced" trial balance is no guarantee of correctness. For example, failing to record a transaction, recording the same transaction twice, or posting an amount to the wrong account would produce a balanced (but incorrect) trial balance.

Financial statements from the trial balance: Now we can probably see that a tentative set of financial statements could be prepared based on the trial balance. The basic process is to transfer amounts from the general ledger to the trial balance, then into the financial statements.

Balance Sheet:

Balance sheet is a statement of financial position of a concern at a given date. It shows the financial position of a concern at a given date of accounting period, because the situation may be entirely different on the following day and indeed, might have been quite different a day earlier.

A balance sheet may, therefore, be defined as "a statement prepared with a view to measure the exact financial position of a business on a certain date.

"It is prepared from the trial balance after all the balances of nominal accounts are transferred to trading and profit and loss account and corresponding accounts in the ledger are closed. The balances now left in the trial balance are either personal or real accounts. In other words, they either represent assets or liabilities existing on the date of closing of accounts.

All these assets and liabilities are displayed in the balance sheet according to certain principles such as :

a. All real and personal account having debit balances should be shown on the assets side of balance sheet which is on the right-hand side.
b. All the real and personal account having credit balances should be shown on the liabilities side of balance sheet, which is on the left-hand side. The excess of assets over liabilities represents the capital of the owner. This figure of capital must tally with the closing balance of capital account in the ledger after the net profit or loss has been transferred therein.

It shows that when real and personal accounts are placed on the opposite sides of balance sheet according to the nature of balances, the assets side should be equal to liabilities side.

As stated earlier and personal accounts having debit balances are called assets; actually at trader's property and possessions as also the debts owing to him (sundry debtors and bills receivable) are assets.

The real and personal accounts having credit balances along with owner's capital are shown as liabilities. So liabilities are the debts owing by a business to third parties and the owner of the business.

Classification of Assets:

Assets have been classified as follows:

a. **Fixed Assets.** The assets of a durable nature which are used in business and are acquired and intended to be retained permanently for the purpose of carrying on the business, such as land, building, machinery and furniture etc. They are also sometimes called as capital assets or fixed capital expenditures or long lived assets. Fixed assets are collectively known as 'Block'.

b. **Floating or Circulation Asset.** Those temporarily held assets which are meant for resale or which frequently undergo change e.g. cash, stock, stores, debtors and bills receivable. Floating assets are again sub-divided into two parts, liquid assets and non-liquid assets. Liquid assets are those which can be readily converted into cash without appreciable loss. Cash in hand and cash at bank are the example of such assets. Other assets which cannot be readily converted into cash, or not without appreciable loss, are called non-liquid assets e.g., stock, stores.

c. **Fictitious Assets.** Those assets which are not represented by anything concrete or tangible. Preliminary expenses, debit balance of profit and loss account are the examples of such assets. These are also called as 'nominal' or 'imaginary' assets.

Classification of Liabilities:

The liabilities of a concern can be classified as given below:

a. ***Fixed Liabilities.*** Those liabilities which are to be redeemed after a long period of time. This includes long term loans.

b. ***Current Liabilities***. Those liabilities which are to be redeemed in near future usually within a year. Trade creditors, bank loan, bills payable etc., are examples of current liabilities.
c. ***Contingent Liabilities***. These are not actual liabilities but their becoming actual liability is contingent on the happening of a certain event. In other words, they would become liabilities in the future provided the contemplated event occurs. If it does not occur, no liability is incurred. Since such a liability is not an actual liability, it is not shown in the balance sheet. Usually, it is mentioned in the form of a footnote.

Form of Balance Sheet:

A balance sheet has two sides-the left-hand side and the right-hand side. These two sides, however, are not comparable with the debit side and credit side of a ledger account because balance sheet is not an account. Words 'To' or 'By' are not used in the balance sheet The left-hand side is liabilities side and contains credit balances of all real and personal accounts and on the right-hand side which is "assets" side, are listed the debit balances of real and personal accounts.

Arrangement of Assets and Liabilities in Balance sheet:

The assets and liabilities should be arranged in balance sheet in some specific order. Arrangement of assets and liabilities in the balance sheet is called 'Marshalling of assets and liabilities'. There are two systems of arrangement of assets and liabilities in the balance sheet:

a. Order of Liquidity.
b. Order of Permanence.

In liquidity order most easily realizable assets are shown first and are followed by assets which are less easily resalable. So, the assets most difficult of realization will be shown last. In case of liabilities, these will be shown in the order in which they are payable the most pressing liability being placed first.

Distinction between Trial Balance and Balance Sheet:

1. Trial balance is the 'means' of accounting process of which the balance sheet is the 'end' because a balance sheet is always prepared from the figures taken out of trial balance.
2. The purpose of preparing a trial balance is to check the arithmetical accuracy of account books; but balance sheet is drafted to reveal the financial position of the business.
3. The two sides of balance sheet are called 'liabilities' and 'assets' sides respectively but incase of -trial balance the columns are 'debit' and 'credit' columns.
4. For completing the accounting cycle, the preparation of balance sheet is. necessary; but the preparation of trial balance is not always necessary. –
5. The period after which a balance sheet is prepared, is normally one year but trial balance is prepared very often and it may be monthly, quarterly or half-yearly.

6. Trial balance contains in it all the three types of accounts viz. personal real and nominal, but balance sheet contains only personal and real accounts.~
7. Generally, trial balance does not contain closing stock but balance sheet does.
8. It is not possible to know the accrued, advance, outstanding and prepaid receipts and expenses from trial balance, but balance sheet discloses such items.

Manufacturing Account:

Some concerns like to ascertain the cost of goods manufactured by them during the year distinctly before they prepare the trading account and ascertain the gross profit. This account is called the manufacturing account and is prepared in addition to the trading account. It has the under mentioned characteristics:

i. Since the purpose of preparation of this account is to ascertain the cost of goods produced during the year, the opening and closing stocks of finished goods are not entered in it ; they will figure in trading account.
ii. In respect of materials it is the figure of materials consumed which is debited to the account. This figure is obtained by adjusting the purchase of materials for the opening and closing stocks of materials e.g., Opening stock of raw materials Add: purchases of raw materials during the year Less: closing stock of raw materials Cost of materials consumed In the manufacturing concern there will always be some unfinished goods or work-in-progress. The cost of work-in-progress at the end of the year is credited to this account, shown in the balance

sheet and debited to the manufacturing account of next year as on opening balance.

iii. All expenses in factory- wages, power and fuel, repairs and maintenance, factory salaries factory rent and rates are debited to this account. Depreciation on machinery is also debited to this account and not to the profit and loss account as is usually done.

iv. Amounts raised by sale of waste or scrap materials are deducted from raw material purchases.

v. Now the difference is two sides of this account will be the cost of goods manufactured during the year. This cost will be credited to manufacturing account and debited to trading account.

The trading account will now comprise only the opening and closing stock of finished goods, the cost of goods manufactured as transferred from manufacturing account and sales of finished goods. The gross profit will be transferred to profit & loss account. The profit and loss account and the balance sheet will be prepared as already explained.

Trading and Profit and Loss Account:

It is the summary of such accounts which effect the profit or loss of the concern. These are prepared by transferring from the trial balance all nominal accounts and accounts relating to goods by means of journal entries called 'closing entries'. All remaining accounts i.e. real and personal, relating to properties, assets, debtors and creditors are shown in the balance sheet. In order to know the overall picture of the effect of these accounts they are grouped at one place. Items' increasing profit (revenue) are put on one side (credit) and those decreasing profits (losses and expenses) un the other side (debit). The balance is either net profit or net loss. This income statement is normally divided into two parts - first part is called trading account and second part is called profit and loss account. The procedure for preparing various accounts is discussed in details in the following pages:

Trading Account:

As already discussed, first section of trading and profit and loss account is called trading account. The aim of preparing trading account is to find out gross profit or gross loss while that of second section is to find out net profit or net loss.

Perperation of Trading Account

Trading account is prepared mainly to know the profitability of the goods bought (or manufactured) sold by the businessman. The difference between selling price and cost of goods sold is the,5 earning of the businessman. Thus in order to calculate the gross earning, it is necessary to know:

a. cost of goods sold.
b. sales.

Total sales can be ascertained from the sales ledger. The cost of goods sold is, however, calculated. n order to calculate the cost of sales it is necessary to know its meaning. The 'cost of goods' includes the purchase price of the goods plus expenses relating to purchase of goods and brining the goods to the place of business. In order to calculate the cost of goods " we should deduct from the total cost of goods purchased the cost of goods in hand.

We can study this phenomenon with the help of following formula:

Opening stock + cost of purchases - closing stock = cost of sales

As already discussed that the purpose of preparing trading account is to calculate the gross profit of the business. It can be described as excess of amount of 'Sales' over 'Cost of Sales'. This definition can be explained in terms of following equation:

Gross Profit = Sales-Cost of goods sold or (Sales + Closing Stock) -(Stock in the beginning + Purchases + Direct Expenses)

The opening stock and purchases along with buying and bringing expenses (direct exp.) are recorded the debit side whereas sales and closing stock is recorded on the credit side. If credit side isJeater than the debit side the difference is written on the debit side as gross profit which is ultimately recorded on the credit side of profit and loss account. When the debit side exceeds the credit side, the difference is gross loss which is recorded at credit side and ultimately shown on the debit side of profit & loss account.

Usual Items in a Trading Account:

(A) Debit Side

1. ***Opening Stock:*** It is the stock which remained unsold at the end of previous year. It must have been brought into books with the help of opening entry; so it always appears inside the trial balance. Generally, it is shown as first item at the debit side of trading account. Of course,

in the first year of a business there will be no opening stock.

2. ***Purchases:*** It is normally second item on the debit side of trading account. 'Purchases' mean total purchases i.e. cash plus credit purchases. Any return outwards (purchases return) should be deducted out of purchases to find out the net purchases. Sometimes goods are received before the relevant invoice from the supplier. In such a situation, on the date of preparing final accounts an entry should be passed to debit the purchases account and to credit the suppliers' account with the cost of goods.
3. ***Buying Expenses:*** All expenses relating to purchase of goods are also debited in the trading account. These include-wages, carriage inwards freight, duty, clearing charges, dock charges, excise duty, octroi and import duty etc.
4. ***Manufacturing Expenses***: Such expenses are incurred by businessmen to manufacture or to render the goods in saleable condition viz., motive power, gas fuel, stores, royalties, factory expenses, foreman and supervisor's salary etc.

Though manufacturing expenses are strictly to be taken in the manufacturing account since we are preparing only trading account, expenses of this type may also be included in the trading account.

(B) Credit Side

1. Sales. Sales mean total sales i.e. cash plus credit sales. If there are any sales returns, these should be deducted

from sales. So net sales are credited to trading account. If an asset of the firm has been sold, it should not be included in the sales.

2. Closing Stock. It is the value of stock lying unsold in the godown or shop on the last date of accounting period. Normally closing stock is given outside the trial balance in that case it is shown on the credit side of trading account. But if it is given inside the trial balance, it is not to be shown on the credit side of trading account but appears only in the balance sheet as asset. Closing stock should be valued at cost or market price whichever is less.

Valuation of Closing Stock:

The ascertain the value of closing stock it is necessary to make a complete inventory or list of all the items in the god own together with quantities. On the basis of physical observation the stock lists are prepared and the value of total stock is calculated on the basis of unit value. Thus, it is clear that stock-taking entails (i) inventorying, (ii) pricing. Each item is priced at cost, unless the market price is lower. Pricing an inventory at cost is easy if cost remains fixed. But prices remain fluctuating; so the valuation of stock is done on the basis of one of many valuation methods.

The preparation of trading account helps the trade to know the relationship between the costs be incurred and the revenues earned and the level of efficiency with which operations have been conducted. The ratio of gross profit to sales is very significant: it is arrived at :

Gross Profit X 100 / Sales

With the help of G.P. ratio he can ascertain as to how efficiently he is running the business higher the ratio, better will be the efficiency.

Closing Entries pertaining to trading Account:

For transferring various accounts relating to goods and buying expenses, following closing entries recorded:

i. **For opening Stock**: Debit trading account and credit stock account
ii. **For purchases**: Debit trading account and credit purchases account, the amount being the et amount after deducting purchases returns.
iii. **For purchases returns**: Debit purchases return account and credit purchases account.
iv. **For returns inwards**: Debit sales account and credit sales return account
v. **For direct expenses**: Debit trading account and credit direct expenses accounts individually.
vi. **For sales**: Debit sales account and credit trading account. We will find that all the accounts as mentioned above will be closed with the exception of trading account
vii. **For closing stock**: Debit closing stock account and credit trading account After recording above entries the trading account will be balanced and difference of two sides ascertained. If credit side is more the result is gross profit for which following entry is recorded.

viii. **For gross profit**: Debit trading account and credit profit and loss account If the result is gross loss the above entry is reversed.

Profit and Loss Account:

The profit and loss account is opened by recording the gross profit (on credit side) or gross loss (debit side).

For earning net profit a businessman has to incur many more expenses in addition to the direct expenses. Those expenses are deducted from profit (or added to gross loss), the resultant figure will be net profit or net loss.

The expenses which are recorded in profit and loss account are ailed 'indirect expenses'. These be classified as follows:

Selling and distribution expenses:

These comprise of following expenses:

a. Salesmen's salary and commission
b. Commission to agents
c. Freight & carriage on sales
d. Sales tax
e. Bad debts

(j) Advertising

g. Packing expenses
h. Export duty **Administrative Expenses.** These include:

a. Office salaries & wages
b. Insurance
c. Legal expenses
d. Trade expenses
e. Rates & taxes
f. Audit fees
g. Insurance
h. Rent
a. Printing and stationery
j. Postage and telegrams
k. Bank charges

Financial Expenses:

These comprise:

a. Discount allowed
b. Interest on Capital
c. Interest on loan
d. Discount Charges on bill discounted
e. Maintenance, depreciations and Provisions etc.

These include following expenses

a. Repairs
b. Depreciation on assets
c. Provision or reserve for doubtful debts
d. Reserve for discount on debtors.

Along with above indirect expenses the debit side of profit and loss account comprises of various business losses also.

On the credit side of profit and loss account the items recorded are:

a. Discount received
b. Commission received
c. Rent received
d. Interest received
e. Income from investments

(j) Profit on sale of assets

g. Bad debts recovered
h. Dividend received
a. Apprenticeship premium etc.

Preparation of Profit and Loss Account:

As already stated profit and loss account is commenced with gross profit or gross loss as ascertained by trading account. Then the profit and loss account is debited with all indirect expenses and losses. This results in closing of indirect expenses and losses account. The profit and loss account is then credited with various incomes and gains accounts by which all these accounts are closed.

Explanation of Certain items of Profit and Loss Account:

1. *Salaries*

Salaries are paid for the services of employees and are debited to profit and loss ac- count being indirect expense. If any salary has been paid to proprietor or partners, it should be shown separately because it requires special treatment at the time of income tax assessment.

2. *Salaries and Wages*

When wages account is included with salaries it treated is as indirect expense and is taken into profit and loss account.

3. *Rent*

Rent of the office shop showroom or godown is an indirect expense and so is debited to profit & loss account. However, rent of factory is debited to trading account. When a part of the building has been sublet the rent received should be shown on the credit side of profit and loss account as a separate item.

4. *Rates and Taxes*

These are levied by the local authorities to meet public expenditure. It being an indirect expenditure is shown on the debit side of profit and loss account.

5. *Interest*

Interest on loan, overdraft or overdue debts is payable by the firm. It is an indirect expense; so debited to profit and loss account. Interest on loan advanced by the firm on depositor investments is an income of the firm and so is credited to the profit and loss account.

If business has paid any interest on capital to its proprietor or partners it should also be debited in the profit and loss account but separately because this item needs special treatment at the time of income-tax assessment.

6. *Commission*

In business sometimes agents are appointed to effect sales, who are paid commission as their remuneration. So this being a selling expenses is shown on the debit side of profit and loss account. Sometimes commission is also paid on purchases of goods, such 'as expense should be debited in the trading account. Sometimes the firm can also act as an agent to the other business houses and in such cases it receives commission from them. Commission so received is shown on the credit side of profit and loss account.

7. *Trade Expenses*

They are also termed as 'sundry expenses'. Trade expenses represent expenses of such a nature for which it is not worthwhile to open separate accounts. Trade expenses are not taken to trading account.

8. *Repairs*

Repairs to the plant, machinery, building are indirect expenses are treated expense and are debited to profit and loss account.

9. *Traveling Expenses*

Unless mentioned otherwise, traveling expenses are treated as indirect expenses and are debited to profit and loss account.

10. *Horse & stable Expentses*

Expenses incurred for the fodder of horses and wages paid for looking after stable are treated as indirect expenses and debited to profit and loss account.

11. *Apprentice Premium*

This is the amount charged from persons to whom training is imparted by the business. It is an income and is credited to profit and loss account. In case apprentice premium is charged in advance for two or three years, then the amount is distributed over number of years and each year's profit and loss account is credited with its share of income.

12. *Bad debts*

It is the amount which could not be recovered by the trader on account of credit sales. It is a business loss, so is debited in the profit and loss account.

13. *Life Insurance Premium*

If the premium is paid on the life policy of the proprietor of the business; it is treated as his drawings and is shown by way of deduction from the capital account. It should not be taken to profit and loss account.

14. *Insurance Premium*

If insurance premium account appears in the trial balance, it stands for the insurance of the business. This is taken to profit and loss account. Insurance premium on goods purchased, factory building, factory machines are treated as direct expense and are taken to trading account.

15. *Income Tax*

In the case of merchant income-tax paid is treated as a personal expense and is shown by way of deduction from capital account. Income-tax in case of companies is treated differently.

16. *Discount allowed and Received*

Discount is a reward for prompt payment. It is belief to show discount received and discount allowed separately on the credit and debit side of profit and loss account respectively instead of showing the net balance of this account.

17. *Depreciation*

Depreciation is a loss incurred on account of use of fixed assets in the business. Generally, it is charged from profit and loss account at a fixed percentage. The students should exercise great care as regards the rate of depreciation. If rate is without words ‘per annum’, then the rate will be taken irrespective of the period of accounts. This is very important when the period of accounts is less than one year. On the other hand, if the rate of depreciation is ‘per annum’ the depreciation should be calculated on the assets with due consideration to the period for which the asset has been used in business during the year. In case of additions to assets during the year, it is advisable to ignore depreciation on additions if the date of additions is not given. Same rule shall hold good for the sale of assets during the year.

18. *Stock at the end appearing in the trial balance.*

It is important to emphasize the rule that balance appearing in the trial balance is taken to one and only one place. It may either be trading account or profit and loss account or balance sheet. Since stock at the end is an asset, it will betaken to balance sheet. On the other hand, so long as there is stock in trade, account for that must be kept open and thus be taken to the assets side of balance sheet.

Adjustments of Final Accounts:

The object of preparing final accounts is to find out the profits earned or losses suffered during a particular accounting period and to present the true picture of final position of the firm. While drawing the final accounts we have taken only those items of income and expenditure that are both earned and received and incurred and paid respectively.

To ensure that the final accounts disclose the true trading results, it is necessary to lake into account the whole of the expenses incurred, whether paid or not, and whole of the losses sustained. Likewise the incomes and gains earned, whether actually received or not, during the period covered by the trading and profit and loss account under consideration must also be recorded.

In mercantile system of accounting, it is essential to adjust different accounts before the preparation of final accounts. It is quite common to adjust expenses paid in advance, incomes received in advance, income accrued but not received, bad debts, provision for bad debts depreciation on assets and soon. Journal entries are passed to effect the required adjustments; these entries are known as adjusting entries.

Usual Adjustments Outstanding Expenses:

Certain expenses relating to a particular period may not have been paid in that accounting period. All such expenses which are due for payment in one accounting year but actually paid in future accounting years or payment of which is postponed are all outstanding or unpaid expenses. All such expenses must be accounted for in that accounting year in which they are incurred, irrespective of the fact whether they are paid or not. In other words, all paid and also unpaid expenses must be recorded in an accounting year if they relate to that accounting year only with a view to ascertain true trading results e.g. if salaries for the last month are not paid, no entry will appear in books of accounts unless these are paid. So profit and loss account in respect of salaries will thus be under charged than the actual expenditure, therefore the profit will be more.

Prepaid Expenses:

The, benefit of some of the expenses already spent will be available in the next accounting year also, Such a portion of the expense is called pre-paid expense; since such expenses are already paid, they are also recorded in the books of accounts of that period to which they do not relate. The result shown by the final accounts of a particular period will not be correct because such expenses relate to future periods. Therefore, such prepaid expenses must be adjusted in the books of accounts to arrive at true profit. Generally insurance, taxes, telephone subscriptions, rent etc. are paid in advance, thus requiring adjustment e.g. Rent paid by x for one year on 1.7.79 when his accounting year is calendar year; thus rent for 6 months will remain unexhausted and will be c/f to the next year.

Accrued Income:

There may be certain incomes which have been earned during the year but not yet received till the end of the year. Income like interest on investments, rent and commission etc. are normally earned by merchant during a particular accounting period but actually not received during that period. Such income items need adjustments before the preparation of final accounts. Such incomes should be credited to that particular income account. At the same time the income so - earned but not received is an asset because the amount is still to be received.

Income Received in Advance:

Sometimes, traders receive certain amounts during a particular trading period which are to be earned by them in future periods. Such incomes though actually received and therefore, recorded

i.e. not yet earned. Such incomes should be credited to the profit and loss account of the year in which these are earned. Therefore, such income though received is not the income but a liability of that period

Closing Stock:

It represents the unsold stock at the end of the year. Closing stock is valued and following entry is passed at the end of the year: Closing Stock account To Trading Account Closing stock at the end appears in the balance sheet and is carried forward to the next year. At the end of the next year it appears in the trial balance as opening stock and from there it is taken to debit side of trading account and thus closed.

Depreciation:

The value of fixed assets diminishes gradually with their use for business purposes. Although this decrease in the value happens every day but its accounting is done only at the end of accounting period with the help of following entry :Depreciation account To Particulars asset

Interest on Capital:

The proprietor may wish to ascertain his profit after considering the interest which he losses by investing his money in the firm. Interest to be charged is an expense for the business on one hand and income to the proprietor on the other hand. Following adjusting entry is recorded at the end of accounting period: Interest on capital a/e To Capital a/c Interest on capital being an expense is debited to profit and loss account and same amount of interest on capital is added to capital.

Interest on Drawings:

As business allows interest on capital it also charges interest on drawings made by the proprietor. Interest so charged is an income for the business on one hand and expense for the proprietor on the other hand. Following adjusting entry is passed at the end. of accounting period: Capital ale Dr. To Interest on drawings a/e The interest on drawings being an income is credited to profit and loss account is shown as a deduction from the capital.

Bad Debt to be written off:

Bad debts are irrecoverable debts from customers, during the course of the financial year. These are recorded as follows: Bad debts a/c To Sundry Debtors a/c It results in the reduction of customers debit balance and addition to the loss i.e. Bad Debts. At the end of the year when the trial balance is drawn, these two accounts show debit balances. The balance on sundry debtors account, thus arrived, is the net balance, after deduction of any bad debts recorded during the year. But after the trial balance is prepared and before the final accounts are drawn trader may find that there are additional bad debts. Such bad debts must be recorded with the same adjusting entry and giving it following effect in ledger and final accounts.

Provision for Bad Debts:

At the end of the year, after writing off the bad debts about whom we were sure of becoming irrecoverable, there may still be some customer balances from whom it is doubtful to collect the entire amount. However, it cant be written off as bad because non-recovery of such amount is not certain. But at the same time the balance in sundry debtors account should be brought down to its net realizable figure so that balance sheet may not exhibit the debtors at more than their actual realizable value. Therefore, to show the approximately correct value of the sundry debtors in the balance sheet a provision or reserve is created for possible bad debts. Such an adjustment entry is recorded at the end of accounting year.

Provision for bad debts is an attempt to anticipate possible losses due to bad debts and to keep aside an amount out of profit to meet the loss estimated in the following years. When the provision for bad debts is created, following entry is recorded:

Profit and Loss A/c Dr. To Provision for bad debts A/c

Some important considerations while creating provision for bad debts:

i. Sundry debtors account should not be credited with the amount of provision for doubtful debts because the loss has not actually been incurred.

ii. Treatment of bad debts or provision for bad debts appearing inside the trial balance. If some balance (credit) is already appearing in provision for doubtful debts account inside the trial balance, it is the previous years unutilized balance of this account. If some bad debts are also appearing on the debit side of the trial balance, these should be transferred to provision for bad debts account, with the help of following entry: Provision for bad debts a/e To Bad debts a/e. It is important to note that, as these items appear inside the trial balance, so these are to appear only in profit and loss account as debtors have already been reduced during the year.

iii. When bad debts and provision for bad debts appear in trial balance, new provision is to be created and further bad debts are to be written off. If already bad debts and provision for bad debts are appearing in trial balance, these should be adjusted and only difference should be taken to profit and loss account.

If bad debts written off plus bad debts to be written off plus new provision for bad debts is more than the credit balance of old provision appearing in the trial balance, the difference should be debited to profit and loss account.

Provision for discount on Debtors:

It is normal practice in trade to allow discount to customers for prompt payment and it constitutes a substantial sum. Sometimes the goods are sold on credit to customers in one accounting period where as the payment of the same is made by them in the next accounting period and so discount is to be allowed. It is a prudent policy to charge this expenditure to the period in which sales have been made, so a provision is created in the same manner, as in case of provision for doubtful debts

An important point to note is that no discount win be allowed on debts that become bad. Therefore, the provision required for discount will be in respect of the other debts only. So the amount of provision for discount be calculated after deducting the provision for bad debts from sundry debtors.

Provision for discount on creditors:

Prompt payment, if made, enables a businessman to receive discount. The question arises whether this discount should be treated as income of the period in which purchases were made or of the period when the payment is made, if both events are in different accounting years, it has been well decided by accountants that it should be treated as income of the period in which purchases are made. So on last date of accounting period if some amount is still payable to creditors, a provision should be created for such probable income and amount should be credited to the profit and loss account of that year in which purchases are made. Following adjusting entry is passed for it :Provision for discount on creditors a/c Dr. To Profit and loss account

Losses by Accidents:

Sometimes a business suffers certain losses not because of trading but because of certain accidents. These may destroy some fixed assets of the merchant. In such a case the asset account is credited and the profit and loss account is debited.

If goods (stock-in-trade) are lost by accident the value of closing stock win be lower than otherwise. This will reduce the amount of gross profit. So the cost of goods lost by accident is credited to the trading account and debited to the profit and loss account. The increase -in gross profit will be neutralized by the debit to the profit and loss account and thus the net profit will not be effected. The entries to the passed are as follows: Loss by accident a/c To

Goods lost by accident a/c

Commission to manager payable on profits:

Sometimes the manager is entitled to a commission on profits.. Such commission may be :

a. Fixed percentage on net profits before charging such commission.
b. Fixed percentage on net profits- after charging such commission.

Such commission being an expense is debited to commission account. However, as it has not yet been paid, so commission payable account is given the credit and finally it is shown in the balance sheet as a liability. Calculation of Commission First of all trading account should be prepared in usual manner and after transferring the gross profit or loss all expenses and incomes should be debited or credited except the commission which is still to be calculated.

Goods used in business:

Sometimes goods purchased for the purpose of resale are used in business as giving them away for charitable purpose or distributing them as free samples. In these conditions purchases account should be credited with an amount equal to the cost of goods used in business and same amount is debited to charity or advertisement expenses account, as the case may be.

Other financial and accounting reports available under the package selected:

With a computer, you can request and receive an in house balance sheet, an income statement, or other accounting reports at a moment's notice. While keeping your checkbook on a computer may not be practical, computers are great for handling complex home financial records. You can get statements on net worth and year's tax deductible expenses within minutes.

Reports, Graphs:

GnuCash has an integrated reporting and graphing module, and comes complete with a full suite of standard and customizable reports, such as Balance Sheet, Profit & Loss, Portfolio Valuation, and many others.

Most of the accounting packages come equipped with accounts payables, account receivables, payroll and general ledger features. Most will also generate basic reports, invoices and keep track of other expenses, assets and small financial items you may want to keep track of from day to day.

CHAPTER ELEVEN

Enterprise Resource Planning (ERP) Software

> "*Payroll accounting softwares are responsible for figuring, documenting and executing the accounts, no matter it is on monthly, biweekly or on the weekly basis. If you are concerning about the cost of these softwares, it depends on the number of employees and clients you are having in your business. There is other factor of deciding the cost of these softwares is the place where the company is located. Here you need to give the tax according to the laws of the state.*"

Operating these payroll softwares requires skilled manpower. If you are not having the proper knowledge about these softwares then you can also hire the professional full time employee to handle your accounts. The payroll accounting software gives you the smoother, faster and accurate results. If you don't want to hire a full time employee then you can get the training related with this software from any expert. This will save the money as you don't need to spend much time with this software.

But it is necessary for you to identify the growing needs of your company. This will help you in getting the software that is flexible enough to accommodate a reasonable amount of work expansion. It is advisable that you should purchase only original and up-graded payroll software for getting the best results.

Accounting software is an ideal choice for a small business owner, large corporate entity or the individual desiring better management and control of their finances and expenses. Accounting software comes in a variety of different shapes and sizes. There are some key functions you should look for when reviewing accounting software. Below is a breakdown of some of the more common features accounting software offers.

- Accounts Payable - Applications handling A/P functions help automate billing and invoicing when you receive them from vendors for purchases you made. You can use A/P software to schedule payments and issue checks to vendors.
- General Ledger - The general ledger application is the primary focus of many accounting software packages. On the general ledger you can collect information from your financial statements, income statements and balance sheets. Cost reporting typically occurs in the general ledger as well.
- Accounts Receivable - In the A/R application you can automatically track outstanding invoices for collection and payment. Most A/R applications provide you with aging reports to help you track payments before they

become outdated.

- Payroll - Payroll applications often coincide with accounting software to enable businesses to keep track of employee pay rates, tax, deductions and even accrued or used vacation hours. You can usually generate W-2s and other important documents using payroll applications.
- Budgeting and Forecasting - Applications handling budgeting and forecasting help you manage your financial transactions and expected budget throughout the year. Look for a program with a planning module if you can to help you plan your finances for the year.

Aside from basic functions including accounts payable and accounts receivable, there are many other useful functions you should look for when buying accounting software. Here are some key applications and features that may help streamline your business processes.

- Purchase Order Tracking - A P/O application can help automate purchasing and keep track of any orders you place with vendors. It will also enable you to automate repeat order processing and help minimize costs associated with product and service expenses.
- Order Entry - This application often referred to as the sales order or order entry application enables you to create invoices for your own products and services. This application is commonly used for businesses that have to maintain large quantities of inventory. You can integrate your sales order application with your accounts receivables application in many instances.
- Point of Sale - A POS system allows you to keep track of sales as easily as you would with a cash register. They

often integrate easily with inventory control or order entry applications.

- Fixed Asset Management - If you have multiple assets including equipment or vehicles you may need an accounting software program that offers specialty tracking such as that offered with a fixed management system. A fixed asset application will allow you to track individual assets and their depreciation and loss details over time so you can account for them during tax season.
- Inventory Control - If you have a lot of inventory for products or goods you may consider an inventory control application to help you track sales and volume of products in inventory.
- Aside from traditional accounting applications like payroll, accounts receivable and accounts payable you may need to investigate accounting software applications that offer specialty features depending on your firms business and industry. There are accounting software programs that offer CPA specific tasks and those that offer specialized solutions for globally based or innovative business processes. Here are just a few unique features of specialized accounting software applications.
- Tax Preparation - Tax preparation applications come in handy for just about any business, but are particularly useful for CPA firms. Most tax applications will print business tax returns and automate annual corporate tax returns processes for both state and federal tax forms.
- Auditing - Auditing applications enable firms including CPA firms to audit clients financial statements and a firms general accounting practices.

- Foreign currency applications - Foreign currency applications can automatically convert currency between different countries. This type of application is useful for businesses operating in multiple countries. Most include up to date and automated foreign exchange rates.
- Project Management - A PM application is often geared toward businesses in the construction industry. This application helps manager track resources and the progress of a specific project or equipment.
- Sales Force Applications - Some applications helps businesses improve performance by automating sales and marketing applications. These solutions generally enable a business to serve the needs of clients quickly hence enhancing customer service. A sales force system often works in conjunction with a customer relationship management application that provides information from sales, marketing and customer service efforts that integrates with traditional accounting applications

The market of accounting software have been increasing at a fast pace. It has gone through takeover and consolidation since the mid 1990s. It has seen great competition with the entry of larger players such as Microsoft and Sage.

The main operation of accounting software is to record and process accounting transactions of a business within its functional modules. Accounting software is all about accounting software system. There are great variations in the cost and complexity of accounting software. An organization can either build its own accounting software or can purchase it from a third party.

There are various functional modules of an accounting software such as they can be divided in to various sections of accounting. The most common of the core modules are as follows:

1. General ledger which is known to be the company's financial "books".
2. Stock/Inventory section keeps track of the inventory of the company.
3. In the Accounts Payable section, the company enters its bills and pays money of owes.
4. In the Accounts Receivable section, money received is entered.
5. Billing is the section where the company produces invoices to clients.

Some of the non-core modules are as follows:

1. In the Debt Collection module, the company records attempts to collect the overdue.
2. The company tracks wages, salaries and related taxes in the Payroll section.
3. In the Expense section, employee business related expenses are recorded.

There are different categories of accounting software which are as follows:

a. Personal Accounting softwares are mainly meant for home users. They are simple and inexpensive with simple functioning such as, managing budgets.
b. Low end accounting softwares are made for small business markets that are capable of serving a single

national market. It is characterized by 'single entry' products.

c. Mid market accounting softwares work well for people with large businesses. These softwares are capable of serving the needs of multiple national accountancy standards and they allow accounting in multiple currencies.
d. High end accounting softwares are complex and expensive business accounting software that are also known as Enterprise resource planning or ERP software.

Business Accounting Software:

In this age of computer technology, everything has become so handy that a click on your keyboard performs all the tasks that otherwise require much labor and patience. Till now before the accounting software, business or financial activities were really a difficult task. It took more than a week to track all the activities related. It required thorough checking of all the papers and calculations. After that it required professionals of this field to estimate the results of profit, loss, utility, balance, payments, resources etc.

Business accounting software specifically deals with business related activities. Business of any kind means a handful of activities of different sections. From production to finance, from input to output, from managers to daily laborers and many other factors play a part in it! The ultimate goal of any business is profit and growth. And that is not possible until and unless you can trace the features that will help you to grow your business. Business accounting software is your rescue in this tiresome job.

It provides you all information accurate, and reflects the flaws or lacks and builds the strategies to help you grow the business.

How is it possible for business software to do this task?

Let's first learn how the business software works. This will make your idea more clear about the benefits of accounting software in the growth of business. The main areas of the software are- General Ledger Devices: Bookkeeping is the primary job of all business accounting software. It makes the job easier and in a click you can access all the data of bookkeeping.

Accounts Payable: This section takes care of bills, payments, debts and other finance related areas.

Accounts Receivables: The accounts of received amount from various sources are maintained well by the software.

Stock/Inventory Maintenance: The main purpose of this area is to keep a record of the stock of raw materials, money, labor and other things.

Billing: All about the bills is maintained by this section.

Like this the business software prepares a ready made data and reading well this data you can take the steps for your business' growth.

a. Sales and Marketing

Sales is not an independent module in ERP Systems, but a logical view of all customer and prospect related activities. Sales functions are an integral part of the business process. As a result, there are no batch or synchronization processes for the back office functionality as is frequently required to integrate CRM and ERP systems

Customer Requests:

ERP Systems/ modules supports automated processing of customer requests such as:

- Information — unstructured requests from web or email sources
- Service — requests to perform a service at a given time and place
- Charge — requests to reimburse costs
- Account — requests concerning a particular customer or vendor order, shipment, invoice or payment
- Warranty — requests concerning a product or service issue
- Help — unstructured customer service requests

Depending on the type of request, it can be automatically converted into a target document (e.g. a quote, order, or invoice). A confirmation email with tracking number can be sent manually or automatically. Optionally assign requests to specific system users for action or follow-up.

By utilizing the tracking number, the Request creator can update information in the Request. Request Management capabilities within CRM ensure timely response, escalation in accordance with a defined process, timescale, and closure.

Requests can also be generated based on the account status (e.g. date of last sale, overdue payment, etc.) for customer service or sales to follow up.

Marketing Campaign Management:

Customer retention is a crucial mission for every company. ERP systems/modules support this by creating mailings or requests for the sales force to follow up. Criteria for a campaign could be last sale, sales volume, products purchased, or a variety of other triggers.

To attract new customers, addresses of prospects can be imported for mailings or other sales follow up.

The effectiveness of marketing campaigns can be measured by the revenue or gross profit generated for each campaign by linking each document (e.g. Invoice or Order) to the relevant campaign at the time of invoice creation. This information is then available within ERP systems/ modules for reporting and analysis.

Customer Profitability Analysis:

Reports can provide insight on revenue and gross profit for specific customers or customer groups. The flexible reporting tool in ERP systems/modules gives you control over several reporting parameters such as the period of time for analysis. Additional reporting options include exporting ERP systems/modules to files for analysis in Microsoft Excel or OLAP tools. The use of 3rd party report writers against ERP systems/modules' transaction data is also supported.

Pre-Sales and ERP Systems:

The pre-sales process encompasses sales activities prior to an order being placed, such as selecting and configuring products and generating quotes. These activities are distinguished by the need for rapid vendor response and a flexible approach to specifying products to meet your customers' unique requirements.

ERP systems like *TechniCon's* CustomCommerce combine comprehensive sales and configuration tools; flexible data structures, a modular architecture and an overall ease-of-use to satisfy this need.

Pre-sales vs post-sales:

Once a sale has been made, quotes need to be entered as orders. Orders need to initiate manufacturing processes. These post-sales activities have typically been the province of ERP systems. As all pre-sales activities will hopefully lead to post-sales processing, it would appear that these functions should also be part of the ERP system.

However, the systemic differences between the pre- and post-sales environments make this problematic. The pre-sales phase is concerned with "what might be." The post-sales phase operates on "what is." ERP systems are designed to be systems-of-record, e.g. what was ordered, what parts need to be manufactured, what accounts are paid or overdue. They excel at managing this type of hard data.

Using ERP systems to generate and store quotes plays against these systems' strengths. Entering quotes that may or may not become orders into the ERP system "*pollutes*" the system's database. Prospects get mixed in with actual customers. Where there are many quotes to one order, the system becomes flooded with unapproved quotes.

With ERP systems like *CustomCommerce*, the sales system is separated from the ERP system. Quotes don't enter the ERP system until they're approved orders.

Sales systems need to be able to present special pricing and product attributes to meet customer requests. Do you add special pricing or a special color into the ERP system for just one quote? Will the sales rep have to wait for an ERP analyst to enter this data?

Even when no special request exists, ERP systems have to process through their massive data stores to generate a quote, resulting in frustrating delays that discourage sales staff from using these systems. Introducing pre-sales and marketing data into an ERP system further burdens the system with extraneous information and creates downstream maintenance problems.

By design, ERP systems sacrifice a level of flexibility and responsiveness to maximize data integrity and reliability. ERP systems/ modules use more flexible data structures and need to track far less data than the typical ERP system, so they're responsive and easy-to-use.

Rigid vs flexible data stores:

To be effective, ERP systems require fixed formats and rigid structures in order to manage the massive amounts of data that they need to store. Data fields such as product descriptions are limited in length, necessitating the use of abbreviations and internal jargon.

This makes these fields poorly suited for online presentation to customers. Abridged product descriptions can lead to order errors and costly returns, especially where customers have to choose between similarly described products.

ERP modules like *CustomCommerce* data fields can accommodate descriptions of any length, so product descriptions can be detailed and targeted to your customers. These modules can also repurpose product descriptions from your ERP system, automatically expanding abbreviations, removing jargon and cleaning up spelling and typographical errors.

ERP systems typically manage individual part data in an item master database, using fixed length, non-configurable SKUs. For configurable products that can offer millions of combinations of options and accessories, a SKU would need to be entered in the item master for each combination.

As only a small percentage of configurations are actually used, the item master typically contains only SKUs for those products that have been ordered. ERP supports customized products, not just SKUs in a catalog. The ERP can substantiate any configuration and generate its SKU.

E-commerce:

ERP system's e-commerce modules provide an online store that is fully integrated with the rest of your ERP data and business rules. This means that you can run a web store without maintaining independent E-commerce and ERP applications, without periodic synchronization or additional complex integration. The web store components utilize cascading style sheets to ensure a consistent look-and-feel within the store and your external web site.

Online Product Catalog:

Users are able to view and search the product catalog. Product images and specifications are stored for each product and can be displayed on the web store at the user's discretion. Hierarchies can be set up in the product catalog to simplify searching using product category or product attributes.

Online Pricing and Availability:

Support multiple classes of customers, such as end-users and trade customers by applying security rules. Security can limit access to selected products or product categories and to particular price lists.

Additionally, you can configure E-commerce to display product availability as either 'available to promise' or the actual inventory quantity.

Online Sales Transactions:

ERP modules enable users to add items to the Shopping Basket via the Product Catalog or web form request. Item quantities can be changed or removed from the shopping basket. It is mandatory to sign on with secure access to retrieve stored customer information. The payment information is then entered or confirmed.

ERP modules support payment processing using Verisign PayFlowPro and AuthorizeNet. Before submitting the payment for authorization, the credit card number can be verified for data entry errors. This ensures that transaction fees are minimized for rejected transactions resulting purely from erroneous data entry.

After receiving the payment confirmation, the order is created and the receipt is displayed together with the authorization code received from the payment gateway. ERP systems optionally send email notifications regarding the transaction to the customer as well as to the web order processing team.

User and Customer Management:

User information can be stored as cookies enabled to allow automatic detection and sign in functionality. Users are required to authorize their email address to reduce the possibility of fraudulent transactions. The system monitors all web requests, then collects web statistics to analyze E-commerce activity, and quickly identifies visitors to the site as well as click counts.

Organizing Data for E-Commerce:

Properly setting up your product data is the key to the success of your sales and configuration system. ERP systems work with individual items in an item master. *CustomCommerce* works with product lines, categories and products.

ERP system uses product taxonomies and classifications to organize catalog structures so that catalogs are easy to browse and products can be quickly located. Taxonomies are structures that organize data into a hierarchy. Hierarchies classify products into product trees that go from the general to the specific, e.g. furniture/seating/task chairs. As users drill down the tree, they narrow their selections.

An arbitrary number of taxonomies can be defined for a single set of data to create customer and industry-specific tree structures. For example, a furniture product tree for a customer with a multi-campus site might reference locations (e.g. main campus/building 3/conference room) to make it easy to select a chair for a specific space.

Point of Sale:

ERP system's Point of Sale (POS) processing enhances retail sales and E-commerce business processes. Unlike stand-alone POS solutions, each sales transaction immediately updates financial, accounting and customer records, providing a broader view of your overall sales activity and product stocking levels.

Customer Information:

ERP system's POS Software supports either "anonymous customers" or lets you capture customer contact information (e.g., name, phone number, address, email). Once you've established a customer account, you have the ability to accumulate transactions made by the customer and to calculate the lifetime value of a customer account.

Flexible Payment Methods:

POS transactions support your choice of payment methods including:

- Cash
- Credit Card or ACH (with online payment processing)
- Invoice On Credit
- Delivery Notice (invoiced later based on customer profile rules)

Sales, E-commerce, Marketing and Accounting Integration

ERP system's POS fully integrates with other activities. You can convert existing Quotes into Orders or convert an Order into a Quote (in case the customer decides not to go ahead with the transaction immediately).

Monitor sales activities by transaction volume, dollar value, product category or customer category over time. Compare POS information across regions, retail locations and sales representatives.

When used in conjunction with E-commerce, customers who order via the web can specify delivery terms, including picking up the goods from your store. Your customers can also view their orders, invoices and track their shipments on-line.

To monitor the effectiveness of your marketing activities, you can reference POS transactions to specific Marketing Campaigns (e.g. via coupons or discount vouchers). This allows you to compare the bottom line results of different marketing channels and marketing alternatives over time.

Working with Marketing Data:

ERP systems are designed to store data that is typically foreign to ERP systems, such as collateral materials, CAD drawings and other non-transactional content.

While ERP systems store the "hard" configuration constraints used for manufacturing, ERP systems like TechniCon systems allow both "hard" and "soft" constraints. Soft constraints include marketing constraints, such as "this product is not recommended for this application, but can be used" or "this product is available, but will be replaced in ten months."

ERP systems restrict the number of fields associated with a product. ERP systems provides enhanced product attribute structure allows unlimited, dynamic additions to the product database. In addition to feature criteria, product attributes can store content such as up and cross-selling information or promotional dates. Product affinities can be defined, e.g. a mounting kit should be sold for every sign and post order.

ERP - Sales Forecasting:

ERP CRM applications can assess all of your sales opportunities and provide you with greater visibility. You have the flexibility to evaluate opportunities at every point in the sales cycle, value each opportunity, determine prospects' time frame for purchase and identify budgets in place for acquiring your product. Using ERP CRM, you can forecast and analyze your sales opportunities by:

- Managing complex, low-volume sales cycles.
- Measuring your sales results against forecasts.
- Refining and analyzing sales data by account manager, region or probability of close.

Combining ERP, Sales, Marketing and Customer Service:

ERP's Customer Relationship Management (CRM) provides your employees with the information and tools they need to deliver an exceptional customer and supplier experience. Whether it is Sales, Marketing or Customer Service, CRM allows you to optimize the time spent on developing and maintaining successful relationships and maximizing opportunities.

Because CRM is embedded into the many of the ERP systems, there is no redundant data entry and it supports complete access to all ERP related data. CRM allows you to catalog information from initial marketing campaigns and sales contacts through quoting, customer orders, production, shipping, invoicing, payment and RMA cycles. CRM enables you to capture, manage and track every interaction with customers and suppliers in one place—putting it in front of your sales and customer service people, right when they need it.

Benefits:

a. Track the entire customer and supplier business relationship in a single centralized view
b. Proactively manage customer needs and opportunities
c. Increase customer service levels
d. Gain an overall view of sales and support activities
e. Automate routine and repetitive tasks such as mass mailings
f. Single database eliminates the need for entry into multiple systems

"CRM makes it simple to track customer information as well as enter and follow-up on sales activity."

ERP - Monitoring Metrics:

ERP BI applications enable you to configure your Enterprise Business System so you can focus on just the key business metrics you wish to monitor. What would you like to know about your business? ERP BI applications help you uncover the answers to key business performance questions. You can access reports on all areas of your business quickly and easily. Get answers to questions like:

a. What are the sales numbers for the quarter?
b. What are the sales numbers by region and sales rep?
c. How much is it costing us to produce each job?
d. Which products are most profitable?

ERP - Demand Forecasting:

Assessing your product demand is critical for capacity planning, purchasing and inventory management. You may rely on historical performance and trends to make future demand assumptions. Yet, storing, reporting and analyzing meaningful data can be complex and time consuming. Too often, key decisions are made on instinct alone.

To gain a quick and accurate forecast for finished goods, key sub-assemblies and parts, Demand Forecasting takes advantage of the sales data within ERP and a powerful statistic engine to help you make better decisions about your medium-term production plans, long-term capacity plans, purchasing relationships and inventory management. With Demand Forecasting, you have the ability to:

- Share forecast data between M2M ERP and M2M SCM planning applications.
- Forecast at the lowest level you want. You can also auto-select parts to forecast and indicate whether you want to forecast at a level below the part/ revision.
- Calculate demand across multiple facilities.
- Access historical sales data by order date, ship date and issues of material to jobs.
- Create an unlimited number of forecasts or history versions.
- Power your forecasts using a robust, embedded statistical forecasting engine that automatically selects the best forecasting method for each part.
- Generate forecasts for tens or hundreds of thousands of parts within a few minutes.

ERP : Accounting and Finance

ERP's *Accounting & Financial Management* applications enable you to efficiently manage and optimize your business operations across multiple companies, divisions, and sites throughout your supply chain. Whether your users are down the hall, around the globe, or both, Ross ERP system is easily tailored to address your specific needs. It spans international markets and support local languages, currencies, accounting and regulatory requirements, enabling you to conduct business anywhere in the world.

ERP's Financial module is a central source of financial information that leverages data from across your enterprise and helps you manage your critical financial processes – from planning through decision-making. Incorporating proven industry practices, it provides the flexibility and functionality to manage even large, complex, or multi-national enterprises in dynamic business environments. It's also tightly and seamlessly integrated with Ross Enterprise's other software solutions to streamline and automate manual processes and deliver the information you need to make informed business decisions across your global supply chain.

The financial management features within ERP Financial module help you manage all your critical accounting functions. From creating a budget and enhancing your cash flow position to processing accounts payable and accounts receivable and preparing detailed financial reports, the ERP financial management tool set helps you carefully manage your bottom line. One can explore the details on the balance of the ERP financial application suite:

1. Budgeting/Cash Flow- Develop budget forecasts based on different sources and plan ahead for your future cash needs.
2. Accounts Payable/Receivable- Pay your suppliers at just the right time and automate the billing process for better tracking and analysis of your revenue streams.
3. General Ledger- Link all monetary functions, such as receivables, payables, payroll, and order costing, for greater visibility and control over your financial activities.
4. Advanced Reports- Create advanced financial reports and drill down into source data for further analysis.
5. Payroll- Integrate your M2M ERP accounting functions with third-party payroll providers such as ADP and other Payroll system.
6. Human Resources- Manage employee relations, government mandates, and ever- changing benefit options with the integrated ERP Suite HR.
7. Progress Billing- Divide your bill into separate increments and still track the whole process to generate needed cash flow.
8. Bank Reconciliation- Monitor all your checking account transactions and streamline your cash management operations.
9. Compusoft Drill Down Tools- Drill down into supporting financial data directly from the trial balance and generate financial reports to meet your specific requirements.
10. FRx Forecaster- Reduce the time you spend on collecting and sorting through spreadsheets and other information from different departments.

ERP - Accounts Payable:

ERP accounts payable keeps track of which suppliers you owe, how much you owe them, and when payments are due. You can even prioritize your suppliers based on negotiated terms and pay them accordingly. ERP accounts payable helps you to:

- Pay your suppliers at just the right time.
- Scan a full set of reports for accounts payable performance analysis.
- Customize accounts payable to fit your unique business needs.
- Post new invoices to one or more shipments from a supplier and/or separate purchase order.

ERP - Accounts Receivable:

- ERP accounts receivable automates much of the invoicing process by being tightly integrated with M2M ERP Sales and Production. After an order ships, the system queues accounts receivable to issue an invoice. ERP automatically transfers information from the shipper and sales order to the invoice, saving you time by eliminating duplicate data entry tasks. ERP accounts receivable allows you to:
- Automate the invoicing process so that you can stay on top of billing.
- Use full accounts receivable analysis tools for tracking and assessing revenue streams.

- Set up your invoices so they match the way you do business.
- Customize your invoices with important messages to your customers

ERP - General Ledger:

The general ledger integrates monetary flow from every aspect of your business and controls financial activities. Information from the general ledger is linked to the accounts receivable, accounts payable, payroll and order costing functions, which are sub-ledgers. Daily postings in these sub-ledgers can be made immediately or on a delayed basis. Since information is shared across all functional areas within the Enterprise Business System, you can significantly reduce manual journal entries. ERP makes your general ledger accurate and precise by enabling you to:

Easily close periods and keep your accounts up-to-date.

- Have full control over which transactions post automatically and which are posted manually.

- Distribute plant-wide expenses to departments or cost centers automatically.
- Plan budgets, account for sub-ledger transactions, and report on financials.
- Review transactions using more than a dozen reports.

ERP - Bank Reconciliation:

To assist you in managing your cash flow, ERP includes the Bank Reconciliation feature, which gives you the ability to monitor all of your checking account transactions within the ERP accounting system.

To streamline your cash management operations, the Bank Reconciliation feature allows you to indicate "cleared" checks, create deposit records and clear deposits in the system.

In addition, you can easily reconcile the differences between cash accounts and bank statements for transactions appearing on the bank statement that have yet to be recorded in ERP accounting system. The Bank Reconciliation feature gives you the ability to:

- Monitor all transactions within a checking account inside ERP.
- Create, track and clear checking account deposits in the system.
- Track which checks have cleared your checking account.
- Reconcile bank statements and checking accounts with ERP

ERP - Advanced Reports:

Reporting is a powerful tool for financial personnel of small and midsize manufacturers and distributors that need financial software applications for analysis and reporting. It provides rapid and flexible financial reporting, consolidation and drill-down capabilities. With the Reporting feature, you can create new reporting relationships without changing the chart of accounts or the way you enter financial data. The Reporting function is a useful tool that:

a. Provides powerful, easy-to-use tools for creating financial reports that show the information you want.
b. Features drill-down capability on any report data to find out the origin of information.
c. Crafts custom reports that you can send to anyone.
d. Imports and exports data from spreadsheets for data processing and statistical analysis.

Advantages of ERP : ERP accounting and financial modules

Flexible Financial Processes Match Your Business

- Delivers flexibility in key areas such as the chart of accounts, currencies, fiscal calendars, balance types, and accounting periods to facilitate local business requirements

– while streamlining global consolidation and analysis capabilities.

- Enables you to create vendor and customer diaries containing information to help you manage your business more efficiently. Diary entries can be set with future progression dates to remind users to follow up on various tasks.
- Spans international markets and supports local languages, currencies, accounting, and regulatory requirements. All multi-currency transactions

provide you with the originating currency value, the base currency, and the conversion rate, allowing you to manage multi-national transactions easily.

Seamless Integration with Other Applications:

- Reduces or eliminates re-keying by automatically creating invoices from sales or purchase orders.
- Reduces or eliminates guesswork and re-keying by sharing data such as payment terms, bank codes, and customer and supplier information across all applications.
- Creates detailed and accurate financial reports, such as profit and loss statements, that are organized by product or job/activity.
- Allocates overhead costs to a specific product based on statistics, and in the same way allocates expenses incurred in the payroll back to manufacturing.

Competitive Advantages:

a. Automates and streamlines your accounting closing cycles.
b. Lowers your per-transaction costs with more efficient operations across finance.
c. Delivers key financial results to business managers electronically.
d. Grows your global business operations in multiple currencies and languages.
e. Improves interactions with suppliers and customers.

f. Eliminates the need for spreadsheets for reporting, budgeting, and costing.
g. Eliminates surprises with increased budgetary control over expenditures.
h. Improves management analysis of your business operations with integrated costing capabilities.
a. Provides insights and improved decision-making across your extended enterprise.

Author

Dr. Anshumali Pandey is a renowned & reliable name in the field of Education, Hospitality, Tourism and Tribal Food. He is a Teacher and Chef by profession, and also an Author, a Business Auditor, and an avid culinary traveller to the Indian Sub continental hinterlands. Dr. Anshumali Pandey is a Hospitality Educator (PhD) who specialises in Higher Education, Office Administration, Pay roll, HR, Labour Laws, Audit, and Procurement & Tender Process. He is an Author with 66 Publications consisting of 48 Books and 3 short stories.

His contribution and research in the field of Tribal Food, Tribal Tourism, Forest Tourism and Village Tourism in the form of research papers have brought several laurels to him. In 2018 the Ministry of Tourism, Govt of Indian duly recognised all this and awarded him with a National Appreciation certificate and memento.

The books written by **Dr Anshumali Pandey** are essentially a banquet arising from an experience of over 25 years of Professional life and have boiled down to crisp and accurate writing on his favourite subjects. Hospitality Sector champion requires to be a specialist in many fields and Dr Pandey is one of them. His knowledge is evident from the spectrum of subjects which he has chosen for his books so far, which ranges from being a specialist chef, to Master of Human resources, to Education and to love for children, and topped with Spirituality. For more than two decades Dr Pandey has lived with his family in Western India in general and the Tribal belt of the union territory of Dadra & Nagar Haveli in particular. Most of his time is consumed in helping and understanding the Tribal and rural population of the region and writing scholarly articles and books on his vast area of interest.

Books written by the Author are –

1. Theory of Indian Cookery
2. Beauty and Irony of Silvassa Tourism
3. A Short Indian Food Story
4. Be Your Own Guide to Indian Cuisine
5. Cookery Fundamentals
6. History of Indian Food (2 Editions Printed)
7. The Great Indian Story Book for Children
8. Personal Budget: Easy Work Book
9. Online Classes Log Book
10. Dictionary Making Work Book for School Children
11. The Lazy Bed
12. Hindu Dharm (हन्दि धरम) (In Hindi Language)
13. Where is my coffee?
14. Your First Job is Never your Last (Volume 1)

15. You are Almost There (Quick Fix Resume and Interview Hacks)
16. Working for the Enemy? - A lesson in Career Management
17. Public Speaking for the Young
18. A Date With Coffee
19. How to be The Best Hotel Front Office Employee
20. Diploma in Food Production, The complete Syllabus
21. Diploma in F&B Service, The Complete Syllabus
22. Diploma in Front Office, The Complete Syllabus
23. The Time to Speak is Now
24. Munshi Premchand (Short Stories in English)
25. The Housekeeping Department, Text Book
26. Hitchhiker's Guide to Trekking in Uttarakhand
27. Uttarakhand, A divine Land for a Reason
28. Bachhon ke liye rochak kahaniyan (बच्चों के लिए रोचक कहानियाँ) (In Hindi Language)
29. Basic Communication Skills of English
30. The Basic Office Organisation Book for Start-ups
31. Hospitality HRM
32. Hospitality Marketing
33. Bakery Ingredients and Tools
34. Human Resource Management for Indian Professionals
35. The process of LAWFULLY operating a Hospitality business in India
36. Indian Classical Sweets: History, Tradition and Recipes
37. History of India's Himalayan Cuisine: Classical Cookery of Kashmir, Laddakh, Jammu, Himachal, Lahaul, Spiti, Garhwal, Kumaon.
38. Vindu: Andhra Cuisine (Part 1 of South Indian Trilogy)
39. Saappadu: Tamil Cuisine (Part 2 of South Indian Trilogy)

40. Sadya: Malayali Cuisine (Part 3 of South Indian Trilogy)
41. South Indian Cuisine - The Researcher's Guide Book
42. The Ramayana for Children and other short stories from Indian Mythology
43. Legends of the Tribal Shiva
44. Third Generation Children's Story Book
45. It's Elementary: The Top Nine Adventures from the memoirs of Dr John H Watson
46. UNITY IN DIVERSITY, The foundation of Indian Tourism
47. The Thar Express: Culinary History of Rajasthan and Gujarat
48. **Basics of Computerized Accounting**

Connect with me: anshumali.pandey@gmail.com
https://notionpress.com/author/337004

Please scan this QR code on you phone to know more about the latest and complete works of Dr Anshumali Pandey

AUTHOR

www.ingramcontent.com/pod-product-compliance
Ingram Content Group UK Ltd.
Pitfield, Milton Keynes, MK11 3LW, UK
UKHW021936190726
13853UKWH00004B/1480